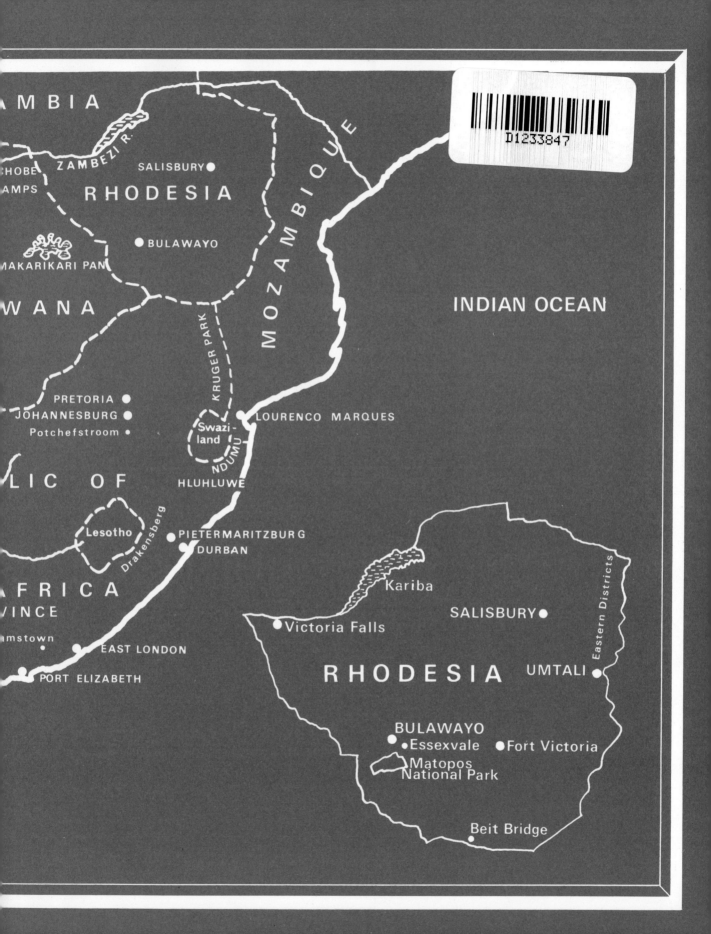

ZAMBIA

ZAMBEZI R.

CHOBE
CAMPS

RHODESIA

SALISBURY ●

● BULAWAYO

MAKARIKARI PAN

BOTSWANA

PRETORIA ●
JOHANNESBURG ●
Potchefstroom ●

REPUBLIC OF

Lesotho

Drakensberg

AFRICA

PROVINCE

Grahamstown ●

● EAST LONDON

● PORT ELIZABETH

MOZAMBIQUE

KRUGER PARK

Swazi-
land

NDUMU

HLUHLUWE

PIETERMARITZBURG
● DURBAN

LOURENCO MARQUES ●

INDIAN OCEAN

Kariba

Victoria Falls ●

SALISBURY ●

Eastern Districts

RHODESIA

UMTALI ●

BULAWAYO
● Essexvale   ● Fort Victoria
Matopos
National Park

Beit Bridge ●

EAGLE DAYS

A study of African eagles at the nest

Peter Steyn

SABLE PUBLISHERS (PTY) LIMITED
SANDTON

To the Memory of my Brother
JOHN

Published by
Sable Press (Pty) Ltd
PO Box 98014 · SLOANE PARK · 2152
Republic of South Africa

© Peter Steyn 1973

First published in Great Britain in 1974 by
Macdonald & Jane's

First published in the Republic of South Africa by
Purnell & Sons (SA)

Design and layout Kenneth Newman

Printed and bound by Creda Press Cape Town

Library of Congress catalogue 73-91015

ISBN 360 00224 2

CONTENTS

ILLUSTRATIONS

FOREWORD

by Leslie Brown

I first met Peter in London and he accompanied me on a two week trip to Scotland to check on the existence of certain suspected Golden Eagle eyries. Since then, I've seen too little of him and we've never really been on that long good eagle safari we've often written or thought about. It has also fallen out that on some of the occasions when we've met since I've not been at my best, and have not been able to live up to my Scottish reputation, gained on a mild eight mile walk on an exceptionally fine day, of being a tough old brute. I've had a slipped disc or something that elongates the twenty years I can give him.

In Scotland I told Peter the story of MacCrimmon, the hereditary piper of the Macleods of Skye who, being an acknowledged master, had many learners sent to him. He was a hard taskmaster; but on one occasion when a lad excelled himself he exclaimed, at least as much pleased as surprised, "The prentice is above MacCrimmon!" While this story admirably illustrated the innate conceit to which all good Scotsmen freely admit (not without reason either), at least I did have the chance to show Peter something of the Golden Eagles in Scotland that were my first love, and to talk to him about other eagles in Kenya that we both knew well. I like to think that our trip helped him in his later studies in Rhodesia to begin with a better understanding of eagles than I had when I began. If I may equate myself with that grand old man of the pipes, MacCrimmon is pleased, but not surprised, at the prentice's progress.

In our time we have studied many of the same species, Wahlberg's Eagle, the Bateleur, Snake Eagles, the Martial and African Hawk-Eagle. Peter's work in Rhodesia has substantially confirmed and enlarged upon my own in Kenya, and I think that the degree of agreement has been a pleasant surprise to us both. Naturally, there are minor differences of habit; but we have both found African Hawk-Eagles bold and easy to photograph. Peter's work has greatly enlarged our knowledge, especially of Snake Eagles, while he is certainly MacCrimmon himself where Tawny Eagles are concerned.

I fancy that much of his knowledge of eagles has been gained as a bye-product of determination to take the best possible photographs of his subjects at various stages of their breeding cycle, whereas I aim to study eagles away from the nest at least as much as their breeding biology. But we have both had those excruciatingly long sits in hides, and know what it means to obtain any photographs at all, much less perfect ones. Nowadays, when I want a good photograph, I ask him; and I am only one up on him with Ayres Eagle, where I can still reciprocate the favour. The photographs illustrating this book will, I am sure, speak for themselves, and demonstrate the patience and skill of a master of this art.

Those who read this book with the care it deserves will find therein many a titbit of new unpublished knowledge, which I hope may only be the forerunner of scientific papers in which the facts will be set out in greater detail – and Peter is no slouch at that either, though he does not pretend to be a zoologist. He denigrates himself rather unnecessarily when he speaks of ''pundits'' and ''authorities''; he is one himself, and I have urged him to get on paper his detailed work at Essexvale and to fill the gaps where needed. He has the patience, the inquiring mind, the powers of observation, and above all the time to make a greater contribution yet. He also enjoys being alone – an absolute essential for an eagle man, which yet need not make him a misanthrope.

Eagles are hated by some people because they eat other things; loved and admired by others for their independence, aloofness, magnificent flight, and manifest power. They are misunderstood birds that have their place in the grand design of nature, and do not do nearly as much harm to human interests as is generally made out. Facts are needed; but even when painstakingly gathered over years by careful objective observers such as Peter and I they are too often ignored by the bigoted, or the vote-seeking political lawmaker. Both Peter and I have been fortunate that in Rhodesia and in Kenya we have been able to study relatively unmolested eagle populations, and thus can flatter ourselves that we have a better idea of their normal behaviour than those unfortunates who can only watch eagles in Britain, America or Europe, where the hand of man is always to some extent against them, and their natural habitat mainly destroyed, altered, or polluted.

I yet hope that someday before I get, as we say in Scotland on passing the allotted span ''Inty the profit'' I may go on a good long safari with Peter. I will willingly put him into hides while I try to find out what the eagle does away from the nest and out of his sight. And round the campfire in the bush, which we both love and is our spiritual home, we shall thrash out, no doubt sometimes at a white heat, the minor differences in our interpretations of eagle behaviour, and concert our knowledge, to the better understanding of the most magnificent birds that fly.

Kenya,
January 1973.

INTRODUCTION

I have spent countless hours watching eagles with undiminished fascination, and the purpose of this book is to convey some of the pleasure I have derived from my many days with eagles over a period of more than twenty years.

I am constantly amazed at the false information spread about eagles. I wish to do no more than "hold the mirror up to nature", for eagles are sufficiently interesting in themselves and do not require embellishment.

Most of what I have written is derived from my own observations, supplemented by reference to the published work of others where relevant (see Bibliography). This book does not claim to be a text-book on eagles, although all information in it has been carefully authenticated. If readers learn a fair amount new to them about the lives of eagles, I hope the process will have been painless, for my purpose remains to communicate my enjoyment of these birds. Should I succeed in this, then it becomes unnecessary to plead for their conservation.

Except for a brief interlude in Scotland, my experiences with eagles have been confined to southern Africa, mainly Rhodesia. However, my eagle days started in Cape Town in South Africa, so it seemed logical to deal first with the two eagle species I knew there. One of these, the Black Eagle, I later photographed in the Matopos in Rhodesia, and my opening chapter deals with this species in both places. Most of the other eagles were studied at Essexvale in Rhodesia where I lived for nine years. Although observations on the various eagles there overlapped, for the sake of clarity, I have used a separate chapter for each species, or group of species, such as the Snake Eagles. Also, rather than hold up the flow of the text by pin-pointing localities, I have included a map of southern Africa to which the reader may refer for the places mentioned.

The majority of the photographs were taken from hides. A hide, or a "blind" as the Americans call it, is simply a structure in which to conceal yourself from your subject. Some illustrations of hides appear in the following pages, and usually each one is adapted to the task in hand. Quite often, if the nest was on a steep slope, it was possible to use my portable ground hide. Sometimes a floor is nailed onto a wooden pylon of the required height, and then a framework is added to this and covered with sacking. At other times, as was the case with one of the African Hawk-Eagles, the hide may be built in the same tree as the nest, if the conformation of the branches permits this. For the Black Eagle a suitable accessible ledge on a cliff is usually required, as well as a head for heights. Ideally, the hide should be built in advance of the breeding season, but this is not always possible. The golden rule is not to cause your subject any distress that might lead to desertion, and each case must be considered on its merits. I have found Crowned Eagles and African

Hawk-Eagles to be very tame, but it does not necessarily follow that all individuals of these species will be so. On the other hand the Bateleur always seems to be extremely wary at the nest, and attempts to photograph it while it is breeding should be avoided.

Generally, a telephoto lens is required to obtain good eagle pictures, the focal length depending on the size of the subject and the proximity of the hide. The camera used to obtain most of my pictures has been a Hasselblad, initially the 1000F model and later the 500C. Quite often I use a 500 mm lens so that the hide need not be placed too near the nest, but with a confiding subject like the African Hawk-Eagle I have used both 250 mm and 150 mm lenses.

I develop and print all my black and white pictures because one cannot expect a commercial firm to give them the care they deserve. It is pointless sitting for eight hours to get pictures, only to have the negatives spoilt by indifferent processing. Happily, colour processing maintains a high standard, so I have been spared the complexities of developing my own colour material.

An invaluable item of equipment is a small tape-recorder of the "Pocket Memo" variety. At times there are spells of rapid activity at the nest when it is impossible to take vital photographs and write; this is when a tape-recorder is worth its weight in gold.

The work most familiar to bird-watchers in southern Africa is *Roberts Birds of South Africa* revised by McLachlan and Liversidge (1970) and so I have followed their common names and nomenclature.

If I were asked why I watch eagles, I would find it difficult to give a simple answer. It may be, as Dryden wrote,

> "There is a pleasure sure
> In being mad, which none but madmen know".

Whatever the case, few people study eagles intensively because a great deal of time is required, as well as considerable physical exertion and discomfort. But the rewards make it all worth it, for to study a creature as magnificent as an eagle at close quarters is something which has to be experienced to be appreciated. In the final analysis, I suppose that I study eagles as a form of escapism, by no means an unhealthy reason. We are all involved in a demented world where values are mocked while man's inhumanity to man, and his disregard for his environment, continue unabated in new and horrifying forms. One wonders whether this is why there is such a marked swing back to nature – it is almost as if man wishes to return to stir the ashes of the primordial fire in his heart.

I think Dryden is wrong, for my eagle days have provided me with a sheet-anchor in a sea of insanity; by watching eagles I have obtained that perfect peace which the world cannot give.

ACKNOWLEDGEMENTS

I am indebted to so many people over the span of years that it would prove an unenviable task to try and name them all here: I can only hope that those not specifically mentioned will appreciate this and understand that I am no less grateful to them.

To begin at the beginning, I must recall Joe Brooks, Bob Lasbrey and "Skippy" Norgarb – the "lightfoot lads" who were the golden friends of my embryonic eagle days, when the bonds of comradeship were forged in our mutual love for eagles and the freedom of wild places.

Then there were those numerous members of the Falcon College Natural History Society who shared my interest in eagles over a period of nine years and helped me in many ways. It is simply not possible to list them all here, but I hope that they will identify the part they played in the pages of this book. To them all, whatever the extent of their contribution, I am deeply grateful.

The farmers of the Essexvale district extended such warm hospitality and kindness to me on my arrival in Rhodesia that I was quite overwhelmed: to Mr. M. V. Rorke, Syd and Beth Longden and their son, Tim, Douglas and Olive-Mary Robinson, Dave and Margie Tredgold, Mike Mylne and his mother, Mrs. Olive Mylne, I owe far more than I can possibly express here.

Archie Brown, Alan Kemp, Nico Myburgh, Terry Oatley, Vic Tuer and Carl Vernon have all given generous assistance in various ways. Michael Stuart Irwin and Viv Wilson of the National Museum in Bulawayo were always ready to help with the identification of prey remains from eagle nests.

During my years in Rhodesia I have been assisted by two African gardeners, Douglas Masuku and his successor Douglas Thebela, who have done about as much eagling as gardening, and their help has proved invaluable.

Val and Eric Gargett and Leslie Brown read the first draft of this book and made many helpful suggestions for improvement for which I am most grateful. Leslie Brown has given me unfailing encouragement over the years, and he has generously contributed a Foreword.

My thanks are also due to Eric Hosking for permitting me to use his ideas on book design as well as the Golden Eagle picture on p.29, and to Ken Newman for help in many ways, not least in the planning and the production of this book.

An "eagle-man" requires one thing more important than anything else – an understanding wife. In this I am singularly blessed. Not only has Jenny never begrudged me a moment of time spent with eagles, but she also patiently typed the manuscript of this book.

1 *An Eagle in the Mist*

The mist swirled between the overhanging cliffs of Skeleton Gorge on Table Mountain as a boisterous gust caught it. For a moment visibility improved, and it was then than I saw it. Framed in the neck of the gully a Black Eagle appeared, rocked slightly as it adjusted its pinions to the rising air, and then faded like a ghost into a world of grey. A small boy, poised on skinny legs on a boulder in the midst of a mossy scree, nearly lost his balance in excitement, but the image had been fixed forever in his mind. He had noted the long broad-tipped wings which tapered as they joined the body, the white "windows" near the wing tips, and the flash of white on its back.

I was eleven at the time, and the incident marked the beginning of an enduring passion for eagles. It was my first eagle, and it had impressed me beyond words. The combined power and grace of the bird, etched against the mist, had struck a responsive chord in my innermost being, and the poetry of eagles was to draw me on from that time forth.

On that day I had been climbing to the top of Table Mountain with my older brother John, from whom I acquired my abiding love of mountains and classical music. Many were the mountains we were still to climb together in the Cape Province and elsewhere in South Africa, and Black Eagles belonged to the world of crags we scaled.

Except for the Lammergeyer (or Bearded Vulture) and the Bateleur, no other large birds of prey I have seen can surpass the powers of flight of the Black Eagle. It will glide past you with effortless ease, one wing tip almost brushing the crags, yet minutes later the same bird is a mere speck in the summit of heaven. Then, folded into the shape of a heart, it will plummet earthwards at breathtaking speed, like a falling stone from a cobalt sky. When collision with the rocks below seems inevitable, it uses its impetus to soar upwards again and loop the loop. At such a time the white back shows to advantage, and spectacular flights of this nature are used for display purposes. I think that if I ever become tired of watching a Black Eagle fly, then I will be weary of life itself.

The first twenty-five years of my life were spent in Cape Town and, apart from the Fish Eagle, the Black Eagle was the only eagle I could watch. Its preference for mountainous areas has ensured its survival in the south-west Cape, and in the late nineteen-fifties I knew of at least four pairs which lived on the mountains of the Cape Peninsula. Another factor in its favour is that, more than any other eagle in southern Africa, it is specific in its prey requirements and takes dassies (hyrax) almost exclusively. A recent study in the Matopos, Rhodesia, revealed that of 1 099 prey items recorded 98,3% were dassies. My remarks may give the impression that

1

My first eagle picture: the female Black Eagle broods her small eaglet at Westlake.

the Black Eagle has escaped persecution, but this is not the case. As a boy I kept a scrapbook of photographs and cuttings, culled from farming journals and the local press, which testified to the fact that it was often senselessly slaughtered. Each new report sickened me beyond measure until, as my youthful fury cooled, I came to realise that the solution did not lie in ineffectual legislation, but in educating the general public in an effort to dispel the prejudice and ignorance which was so prevalent. But while the death of an eagle is brought about by the mere tightening of a finger on a trigger, or the laying down of poisoned bait, or the slam of the jaws of a trap, a case for the defence of eagles can only be established after many years of painstaking study. I would be the first to admit that I have derived untold pleasure from my days with eagles, but there was always the more serious objective of gathering unbiased evidence on their lives.

I first studied a Black Eagle's nest, with some of my school friends, in the mountains above Westlake overlooking False Bay. We had known of the nest for three years, but it was considered inaccessible and offered no vantage point from which photographs or observations could be made. Then, in 1954, the birds were found building a new nest nearby on an open ledge. Not only was it accessible, but there was also a small cave in which we could build a hide. The nest was 18 metres from the bottom of the cliff and some 30 metres from the top, and we approached it from above without ropes. This was scarcely sound mountaineering, and I shudder when I think back on it now. However after our first descent, which was without mishap, we thought nothing of it thereafter.

As soon as the first chick hatched, we blocked the mouth of the cave with a framework of poles which we covered with hessian. The female was extraordinarily tame, and while we were hammering nails in place she came back to brood. There she remained, although we were in full view as we worked on the hide. Then, when we left, she allowed us to pass within five metres of her on our route back to the top of the cliff.

Next day we returned to take photographs, and the female arrived to brood her downy eaglet as soon as we were inside the hide. After ensuring that she was quite at ease, I carefully set up my antiquated Agfa ¼ plate camera which had a 13,5 cm lens. As the female brooded placidly, surrounded by the carcasses of five dassies, I took my first eagle photograph. Looking back, I realise how ineffectual my equipment was. Yet the thrill of that first attempt at eagle photography has never left me, and my distant picture of the bird on the nest always fills me with the deepest nostalgia for those early days.

The second eaglet hatched some four days after the first. We found it in a weakened condition and fed it up on pieces of meat from a recently killed dassie until it could take no more. However, on our return two days later, it lay dead with one side of its head severely pecked. This was my first experience of the fratricidal strife occurring among a number of eagles. It is known as the "Cain and Abel battle." The Black Eagle normally lays two eggs, incubation begins as soon as the first egg is laid, and the second is usually laid about three to four days later. This gives the first-hatched chick a considerable advantage over its sibling and, as soon as the latter

A Black Eagle banks past the Westlake eyrie and shows its characteristic flight pattern.

4

dries out after hatching, it is continually pecked and hounded round the nest. The female eagle is usually present during these encounters, but she makes no attempt to intervene. At mealtimes, the larger eaglet receives all or most of the food which is offered. Gradually the strength of the smaller eaglet ebbs, until it dies from a combination of hunger and injuries.

There is no published record of a Black Eagle raising two young together under natural conditions. Many ideas have been advanced as to why this should be so, but no satisfactory answer has been found. The obvious explanation that has been put forward, namely that there is insufficient food for two eaglets, is not borne out by the facts. At the stage when the smaller eaglet dies there are often several dassies on the nest. Experiments in the Matopos have shown that if the second eaglet can be artificially fed, and grows faster than the first eaglet, it will be dominant and may even kill the older chick. All that may be said at present is that the killing of the smaller eaglet by the larger is instinctive and invariable, and I rather wonder whether we will ever progress beyond this simple statement of fact.

I made regular visits to the Westlake nest to check on prey and the growth of the eaglet. I was still at school at the time and, except in the holidays, only week-end visits were possible. Also a journey to the nest involved a round trip by bicycle of 25 kilometres. Fortunately, a track made by the Forestry Department gave access to the higher slopes of the mountain below the nest. One seldom saw people up there, and it was a wonderful escape from the suburban existence which chained me during the week. Recently a full width tar road has been laid like a whiplash across the mountain below the nest, and in the name of progress people spill from their cars to despoil the mountainside.

From the measurements made that year I learnt about the pattern of growth common to all eagles I have subsequently studied. In the early weeks the eaglet increases rapidly in weight, and, at the same time, it acquires a second coat of down much thicker than the fine down it has at hatching. The growth of bill, legs and feet progresses rapidly until about half way through the fledging period, after which there is little advance. Once this stage is reached, the eaglet is able to stand and feed itself. Conversely, feather development only starts when the eaglet is five weeks old, and then it progresses rapidly. At the period of maximum feather development there is a marked drop in the rate of weight increase, which results from the energy required for rapid feather growth. Towards the end of the fledging period there is little increase, and usually there is an actual loss in weight; this coincides with the "hardening" of the eaglet in the final stage before it leaves the nest at about 91–98 days.

Adult behaviour is linked to the eaglet's development. Initially, while her offspring is weak and helpless, the female is in almost constant attendance at the nest, and her activities are divided between brooding and feeding the eaglet. Occasionally she will leave the nest for brief periods to soar with the male, and quite often she returns with a spray of green leaves to line the nest. The male's part in these early days is vital; he brings prey for the growing eaglet as well as some sprays of green leaves. As its feathers start to grow, the eaglet is left unattended for longer and longer periods, until adult visits to the nest are primarily concerned with the delivery of prey.

5

A Black Eagle with a six week old eaglet at its nest in the Matopos.

The best time to photograph eagles is when they have a small chick in the nest, preferably from a hide constructed well in advance of the breeding season. At the Westlake eyrie, once we had obtained our pictures in the early stages, we usually had a long wait before an adult brought food. The early period is also full of interest; apart from the female's almost constant presence there is always the likelihood of a visit by the male, when both birds can be photographed at the nest. One of the highlights for me is to watch the feeding of the small eaglet. With her massive bill the female rips off a small piece of flesh, cocks her head to one side, and holds the morsel just in front of the chick's bill. I have never failed to be fascinated by the contrast between the downy helplessness of the eaglet and the power of the parent with her magnificent eye set beneath the projecting yellow "eyebrow". And, although she can crush the life out of a dassie in a paralysing instant, her care of her chick is every bit as solicitous as that of a farmyard hen for her brood.

The weekly visits to the nest revealed a distinct change in the reaction of the adults to our presence. At first the female flew round anxiously, and often the male came to join her. On two occasions she settled at the top of the cliff and gave vent to a musical scream which I rendered as "Quee-ow" in my notes. It was one of the few occasions when I have heard a Black Eagle call, for they are normally remarkably silent birds. As the eaglet grew we saw less and less of the adults, and if they did appear they merely soared in the distance. At no time during our study was there any suggestion of an attack, nor has there been a record of an attack in the Matopos where a survey team has undertaken hundreds of visits to more than fifty nests.

I remember particularly one halcyon August afternoon when we visited the Westlake nest. After measuring and photographing the eaglet, we sat on the nest ledge beside it for some while before climbing back up the cliff. It had rained that morning, but now the sun shone full on us as we sat there. The air was like champagne, and we could see every detail of the Hottentots Holland mountains 30 kilometres away across the Cape Flats. Then, just as we were about to leave, the parents made an appearance in the distance and gave us a display of aerobatics which I shall never forget; they dived and looped and soared, the sun flashing like a heliograph on their white backs as they twisted and turned.

The eagles did not use their accessible alternate site again the following year, and apart from a few desultory attempts to repair their original nest we saw little of them. However, that year was notable for the fact that the "inaccessible" site was reached at last, after some extremely difficult climbing. The nest was even more massive than it appeared from below, rising chest high from its base and measuring a metre across the top. In fact, it was built up to such a height in the embrasure that there would have been little head room for the birds when they stood upright on the nest. We felt that this was inhibiting them from using the nest, and so we pulled a considerable number of sticks off the top of it; the largest of these was a metre long and six centimetres in diameter. Our efforts were rewarded, for the birds used the nest the following year, and with a newly-acquired telephoto lens I was able to obtain a number of flight pictures from the ledge below.

We had found that the Westlake eagles preyed exclusively on dassies, but I was anxious to visit an eyrie in a country area, preferably where sheep were farmed. Such a site was found in 1958 on a sandstone cliff at the head of De Hoop vlei in the Bredasdorp district about 140 kilometres from Cape Town. Although distance ruled out regular visits, we made a number of inspections from time to time over a period of three years. One year we found two young and an infertile egg on the nest, a rare case of a clutch of three for this species. Beside the chicks lay the carcasses of three large dassies, yet another instance of the superabundance of food at this stage of their lives. When we returned to the nest a few weeks later, there was a single eaglet. Although we found only dassies in this nest, our visits were too infrequent to establish that this was all they preyed on. However, had we found a lamb, this would not necessarily have been damning evidence, for a number of eagles, including the Black Eagle, will feed on carrion at times, and in certain areas of Scotland the Golden Eagle feeds to a large degree on carrion.

The De Hoop pair successfully raised an eaglet each year between 1958 and 1960, and we ringed all three. Although the 1960 juvenile came to a tragic end, it yielded some important information. It left the nest at the beginning of October, and it was shot at the end of June the following year near Mossel Bay. This was 180 kilometres east of its nest and indicated that juveniles may wander widely once they become independent of their parents.

A few kilometres from the De Hoop eyrie was the Potberg kloof where there was a colony of Cape Vultures, the southernmost breeding population in South Africa. The situation was ideal for the birds because two steep cliffs formed a funnel where there was always an updraft that enabled them to manoeuvre to their nest ledges on the shady side of the kloof. I never tired of watching these massive but graceful birds coming in to land. An incoming parent would glide in a wide arc until it was lined up on its nest, then lower its legs and draw in its wings to achieve a sudden decrease in height. Finally, having dropped below the level of the nest, it would sweep up to land. Once, using a fast film in the shady conditions, I managed to capture an alighting bird in an archangelic pose. Sometimes landings misfired, often with ludicrous consequences. A misjudged approach, and a bird would land on slippery sloping rock short of its nest; there followed a frantic scrabbling of feet and flapping of wings, but gradually it would slide backwards, like a man on a greased pole, before leaping sideways to glide off and attempt a new approach. I spent a great many hours over the years watching those vultures, but my wonder at their soaring abilities never palled.

In the Potberg kloof there was a pair of Black Eagles that had a nest larger than any I have seen, except for one in the Matopos. It could not be reached, but from the ledge below I estimated that it was not less than two metres in height. Although the Black Eagle is one of our largest eagles, the pair in the kloof were dwarfed when they soared amongst the vultures. I never saw any evidence of friction between the two species, but I know of a reliable case in Botswana of a Black Eagle preying on downy Cape Vulture chicks. Below the Potberg nest we found only the skulls of dassies.

The vultures and eagles shared their domain with a number of smaller birds of

A Cape Vulture in an archangelic pose as it alights at its nest at Potberg.

prey, and these added pleasure to our visits. We recorded Peregrine Falcon, Rock Kestrel, Jackal Buzzard, Red-breasted Sparrowhawk and Gymnogene. The air currents there seemed particularly attractive to White-necked Ravens, and I have seen a gathering of twenty or more soaring amongst the vultures. The solitude of that remote kloof had cast its spell over me, and it was the last place I visited before leaving South Africa.

My next experiences with Black Eagles took place in Rhodesia where I went to settle in 1961. Some 35 kilometres south of Bulawayo there begins the rugged boulder-strewn world of the Matopos. It is an awe-inspiring area of scenic magnificence. Massive granite outcrops dominate every vista, and boulder is piled on boulder as if by the whim of a playful giant at the beginning of time. Not satisfied with this, he daubed them with ochrous tints and plastered them with lichens. Huge pothole caves he gouged out too, where later little Bushmen came to adorn the walls he had forgotten to paint. Wild fig trees cling to sheer rock faces from which they push down weird roots like green snakes to the earth below, and in the gullies the peeling paper bark of *Commiphoras* flutters in the merest murmur of wind. Klipspringers stand on stiletto toes atop rounded boulders, while dassies people the crevices and bask on ledges.

This is the domain of the Black Eagle, and here lives one of the most concentrated populations of any eagle species in the world. When Game Ranger Ron Thomson first plotted 35 eyries on a map of the Matopos in 1959, he little realised that he was sowing the seeds of one of the most remarkable pieces of eagle research ever undertaken. Ornithologist Carl Vernon used Thomson's work as the basis for a survey project in which he was the guiding force for two years, and he enlisted the aid of Bulawayo members of the Rhodesian Ornithological Society. One of these was Valerie Gargett, a house wife and mathematics teacher. When Carl left Bulawayo she somewhat reluctantly agreed to continue the survey, and on retiring from teaching she began to study Black Eagles on a full-time basis; now she can hardly be kept out of the Matopos. She continued to be helped by her survey team, which was drawn from men and women in all walks of life. These week-end bird-watchers shared out an area of 614,4 km² (240 sq. miles) in which there were 55 pairs of Black Eagles; this gave a density of one pair per 10,08 km² (4,4 sq. miles). Few people realise, as they stand beside the simple grave of Cecil John Rhodes, that the eyries of six Black Eagles are visible from that point. The work continues, and Val has published a number of important scientific papers. No comparable study exists, and the work of amateurs has achieved international recognition.

The Matopos area is not only notable for its Black Eagle population – it would be unique for this alone – it also supports a wide variety of other birds of prey. Of the seventeen species of eagles occurring in southern Africa, fifteen have been recorded there at one time or another, and the majority of them are breeding residents. Secretary Birds and vultures are found there, too, in addition to some twenty smaller raptor species and five owls. For the raptor enthusiast the Matopos area is paradise indeed, and the possibilities for research are unlimited.

While I was teaching at Essexvale, a journey to the Matopos would involve about 320 kilometres of motoring. Nevertheless, over the years, I was able to spend a

A female Black Eagle feeds her downy eaglet at a Matopos nest.

A Black Eagle returns to its nest with a spray of green lining.

A Black Eagle's nest showing the cup lined with green leaves.

12

Members of the Black Eagle Survey team descend to a nest in the Matopos.

The rocky habitat of the Black Eagle in the Matopos.

13

A six day old Black Eagle chick viciously attacks its day old sibling: a dassie lies behind them and could supply them both with food for several days.

A thirteen day old eaglet attacks its ten day old sibling which has been returned to the nest after being hand reared: it was immediately removed.

14

This series shows the development of a Black Eagle chick: here it is a week old.

At five weeks the feathers start to push through the down.

By eight weeks it is fully feathered.

15

fair amount of time in the Matopos. Val was generous, as was Vic Tuer, another member of the survey team, who permitted me to use his remarkable hides. It usually requires considerable courage to reach one of Vic's Heath Robinson angle-iron constructions, and one is left wondering how he transported the material and erected it in the first place. The first Black Eagle I photographed in the Matopos was from a hide of his built in a tree growing on the cliff face nine metres from a nest. The photographs were successful, but I omitted to take a cushion with me and I had to perch on an iron cross-piece for several hours.

Apart from that first nest, I have photographed at four other Black Eagle eyries

A female Black Eagle feeds her month old eaglet off a dassie which is clasped in her massive talons.

A Black Eagle alights with green leaves and reveals the striking pattern of white on the back.

in the Matopos. Some sites were more suitable for photography than others, but the pictures obtained over the years built up a composite picture of the home life of this species, and the illustrations accompanying this chapter have been selected from hundreds of negatives. It would be repetitive to describe the long hours spent in various hides; it is enough to say that I have never tired of watching this magnificent species at close quarters, and I know I never will.

Twenty-five years have passed since I glimpsed that first eagle in the mist, yet the image remains ever vivid in my mind, for it symbolises the wild freedom which kindled the fire of my admiration for eagles.

17

2 *The Call of the Fish Eagle*

The sun's rim dips and touches the horizon. A molten ball is bisected, peeps for a while over its distant barrier, and is gone. In the silent sky the hanging clouds are suffused with pink as the road of light on the dark water below fades from crimson to copper. In contorted statuary the grotesque shapes of dead trees are starkly etched against the fading gleam of evening. Suddenly, a ringing cry peals across the black sounding-board of water to be taken up a kilometre away in muted reply. This is the call of the Fish Eagle which epitomises the wild freedom of Africa, and the haunting voice is something special to those who cherish the unspoilt areas that still remain.

The scene is set on the Chobe River in Botswana, but it could be anywhere in Africa where the ubiquitous Fish Eagle occurs. Of all African eagles this species is the most widely known, and its striking white head, breast and mantle, offset against black wings and chestnut underparts, render it easy to identify. For its appearance alone it would be an eagle of note, but when this is combined with its call it becomes spectacular.

I well remember standing in front of the Fish Eagle cage at London Zoo, where they shared their perpetual imprisonment with other African eagles in adjoining cages. It depressed me to see such fine birds in sterile captivity, but despite this they managed to evoke a mood of nostalgia for Africa in me. As I stood there, one of the Fish Eagles threw back its head to call, and I waited in keen anticipation. However, instead of its usual ringing cry, all that issued forth was a dismal croak, and the bird probably had laryngitis from a surfeit of smog. I left in disgust.

The main pair of Fish Eagles that I studied in the Cape nested beside Zeekoe Vlei on the Cape Flats. One could see the cliff on which the Westlake Black Eagles bred in the distance, and three kilometres away the sea rolled up the white sands of False Bay. With the help of my friends Joe Brooks and Archie Brown, it was possible to keep a record of the breeding of this pair during the years 1953–1964. This is the longest breeding history ever established for this species, and some valuable information on clutch size, hatching success, replacement rate of young etc. was obtained.

In addition to the Zeekoe Vlei pair I knew of three other nest sites, one in the Cape Point Nature Reserve, another on the Berg River in the Hopefield district and a third at Bredasdorp not far from the Potberg vultures. This last pair bred in a deep kloof, and once they chose an unusual site on a slab of rock jutting out from its side. Unfortunately, because of the travelling involved, visits to these other sites were infrequent.

During the twelve years that we had the Zeekoe Vlei pair under observation they used four different nest sites. Sometimes they bred for several years in the same

A pair of Fish Eagles in the Chobe Game Reserve: the much larger female is on the right.

19

A Fish Eagle in flight.

nest, while on other occasions they moved to a new site each year. One nest was in a clump of pine trees, and the others were situated in a plantation of eucalyptus nearby. These trees were not easy to climb, and Joe and I scaled them with the aid of large nails driven into the main trunk. We started a hide at one nest, but abandoned our attempt before completion when it became clear that the birds were uneasy about it. Some years later they used this nest again and I concealed my Agfa ¼ plate camera in some of the sacking which still remained on the hide. After cocking the shutter and attaching fishing line to the release mechanism, I made the long descent, threading the line through eyelets I had screwed into the trunk on the way up. Then I waited in a hide on the ground from which I could just see the nest. I could hear the birds calling to each other for a while, and then their cries ceased. After a twenty minute wait, a clatter of wings announced the parent's arrival on the nest, and my

The female Fish Eagle returns to her eyrie near Zeekoe Vlei.

heart thumped as I gave the line a gentle tug. I could not hear the shutter click at that distance, and was assailed by doubts as to whether it had gone off, or whether I had inadvertently tripped the mechanism on my way down the tree. The two eggs were near hatching at that stage, so I left the bird to incubate for three hours before emerging from the hide to retrieve the camera.

That night I developed the film and trembled as I held the negative up to the light. My picture had been a complete shot in the dark, and chances of success were slight; thus my delight may be imagined when I discovered that the bird had not moved and had been perfectly posed at the moment of exposure. I do not enjoy remote control photography, which is so impersonal to my way of thinking, but the portrait obtained that day still remains one of my favourite pictures.

Two young duly hatched, several days apart, and I made weekly visits to the nest to weigh and measure the surviving eaglet. We had removed the smaller eaglet in a weakened condition, but our attempts to rear it failed. The extent of the Cain and Abel battle in this species is not clear, and further research would be well worth while. The Fish Eagle quite often raises two young, and I knew of three cases over the years at Zeekoe Vlei. On one occasion all three young hatched from a three-egg clutch and survived together for at least two weeks; then one disappeared and the remaining two flew successfully. However, sibling aggression does take place, and I once saw a smaller eaglet subjected to a fierce attack; unfortunately the outcome was not known because both chicks disappeared a few days later. Our present knowledge of the Cain and Abel fight in this species is inconclusive; it probably explains the rearing of a single eaglet where two hatch, but two young are raised sufficiently often to indicate either that aggression does not occur at times, or that onslaughts are not necessarily fatal.

The eaglet I studied that year left the nest between its 70th and 77th day, and two months later I found that it was still under parental care. In the initial stages it used the nest as a feeding point, and this stresses the necessity for regular checks towards the end of the fledging period; it would be an easy matter to find the eaglet on the nest and assume that it had not yet flown. Another important point is that inspections of the nest should be carefully made in the last two weeks, because the eaglet may leave the nest prematurely if provoked in any way. It is best to ring eaglets just after they are half grown when their legs are virtually fully developed.

During my visits to the nest I kept a record of all food found – by no means the actual total brought – and by the end of that year's study there was a tally of fifteen mullet, a sea barbel and four carp. The mullet and the barbel could only have been obtained from the sea three kilometres away, and we found that the pair at Cape Point and Bredasdorp also fished in the sea. To those who have no knowledge of the species except on inland waters, this will explain the Fish Eagle's original name, now sensibly allowed to lapse, of Cape Sea Eagle. In another year a few "platannas" were found on the nest; these are the frogs used extensively for dissection by zoology students, but they are better known for their role in the "frog test" for pregnancy. At the Berg River nest we recorded a terrapin and a young Coot as additional items of prey brought to an eaglet.

This unusual Fish Eagle's nest was built on a finger of rock projecting from the side of a kloof.

A week old Fish Eagle chick beside a mullet which has been caught in the sea nearby.

23

The inside of the Fish Eagle's foot is rough and spiky, an adaption for holding its slippery prey. Sometimes they capture fish too large to lift, and then they paddle themselves to the shore using their wings. One remarkable case on record is of a bird seen floating with the current down the Zambezi River. An angler cast over it, reeled it in, and found to his amazement that it had a leguaan firmly in its clutches, while the tail of the lizard was wrapped round the eagle's wing, thus preventing it from taking off or "rowing" itself to the bank. It is difficult to guess the outcome of this apparent impasse, but I have heard it said that if a Fish Eagle catches too big a fish it will be dragged under, like Ophelia, to a watery grave. However, I have yet to hear of one of these tales being properly authenticated.

Besides capturing their prey in open water, Fish Eagles will readily take dead or stranded fish when available. Other aspects of their diet are less well known, and they also prey on adult and young waterbirds; in one incident described to me a young Pygmy Goose was snatched off the water from beside its parent before she could shepherd it into the reeds. They will raid heronries and take nestlings, and in East Africa they kill flamingoes. At the other end of the scale one swooped down and took a tiny Malachite Kingfisher which was caught in a bird ringer's mist net. Piracy is another method of obtaining food, and they will relentlessly harry other fish-eating species such as cormorants, herons, storks, pelicans and the Osprey to make them disgorge or relinquish their food. Perhaps most distasteful of all, for those who believe in the "nobility" of eagles, is the fact that they will also feed on carrion. I remember one particular instance, in the Hluhluwe Game Reserve in Zululand, where a Fish Eagle was feeding with an assortment of vultures on the putrid remains of a rhinoceros.

The Fish Eagle has been intensively studied in East Africa by Leslie Brown where he has concentrated particularly on a population study, and it is clear that they will nest in close proximity in favourable areas. In the south-western Cape Fish Eagles are rare, and I was pleased to know of four pairs. An area which would repay further study, however, is the Chobe National Park in Botswana. On a recent visit in July, when they were nesting, there were 38 pairs along a 55 kilometre stretch of river. Young birds leave the nest in drab brown plumage and take about four years before they achieve full adult coloration; thus it is an easy matter to identify immature birds, but we saw only two during a careful census of the area. One can only assume that juvenile birds disperse widely before the onset of the following year's breeding.

One of my last memories of the Zeekoe Vlei Fish Eagles was when I went for a farewell row with the other members of my university crew. As we pulled up the last stretch to the clubhouse in the dusk, the familiar clear call rang across the water. I could not have wished for a more fitting valediction.

3 *Interlude in Scotland*

Table Mountain wore a shawl of grey cloud as the "City of York" throbbed its way into the swells off Cape Town at the start of our voyage to England and I leant against the rail to watch various petrels and shearwaters. One of my favourites was there, the tiny Storm Petrel, and I noted its erratic flight in the troughs between the foam-capped waves where, from time to time, it would paddle its feet on the surface of the water as it flew. With its black coloration, haphazard flight and small size, it looks more like some freak species of marine bat than a bird.

Soon five Wandering Albatrosses came to follow the ship and they remained with us for the next three days. No bird I know can match the flight of the Wandering Albatross; even my beloved Black Eagle becomes ordinary by comparison. The downwind sweep and turn, with long wings shearing the waves, has a mesmeric effect on me, and I have spent countless hours watching them with undiminished fascination.

One of the most memorable events during our stay in England was a visit to the world-famous bird-photographer Eric Hosking, whose magnificent pictures I had admired from the time I started to photograph birds with a "Baby Brownie" at the age of thirteen. Although he was in the midst of processing hundreds of negatives and prints in his darkroom after returning from an expedition to Hungary, he generously devoted a whole afternoon to answering my many queries on photography. I owe a great deal to him for the advice and encouragement he gave to me, a complete stranger, that afternoon.

We were based in London during our stay, but despite a number of bird-watching trips to various country areas and bird reserves I was becoming increasingly depressed by the lack of birds of prey to be seen. This particularly strikes the visitor from Africa, for not only is the variety of raptor species in England limited, but some, like the Peregrine Falcon, had been decimated by the indiscriminate use of pesticides. I had not been able to range as far afield as Scotland, so the bird I wanted to see above all else – the Golden Eagle – had eluded me. Here was a species better known by name to the general public than any other eagle in the world, and from my boyhood I had pored over illustrated books on it until I think I knew almost every published picture of the Golden Eagle taken in Scotland.

The solution to my dejection arrived one day at the door of our Knightsbridge flat in the shape of Leslie Brown, the world's leading authority on eagles. We had corresponded regularly and he had given me constant encouragement. His own research on raptors, particularly eagles, had been carried out mostly in Kenya, but he had also devoted much of his leave time over the years to studying Golden Eagles in his native Scotland. In our last exchange of letters we had made a tentative arrangement to meet in London to talk eagles should our dates there coincide.

Leslie returned to dinner the following evening, and he asked me to consider accompanying him on a trip to Scotland. My wife had no hesitation in urging me to go, for she realised that I would probably never have a similar opportunity again. We spread a large-scale map of Argyll on the floor and Leslie explained the object of the trip. In a previous survey he had filled in many Golden Eagle eyries on the map, but he was certain that a fair number had yet to be located in his defined census area. He marked all the known nests with pennies, and then proceeded to pin-point where others should exist. We soon ran out of coins, and at the end of the exercise the map was an interesting pattern of small change, sugarlumps and coffee spoons. Leslie explained that it was not so much food supply, but rather territory and availability of nest sites, which determined an eagle population in a given area. The proof of this was to be established after a great deal of walking, and almost all the sugarlumps and coffee spoons turned into actual nests. It put a new dimension into my thinking on eagles, and was to stand me in good stead during my future eagle studies in Rhodesia.

During the day before our departure Leslie swept in and out of the flat to deposit various supplies. He had acquired a second-hand Bedford ambulance which had been converted into a dormobile, and this was to be our home. The following morning we set off in the "Snail" as we had christened it, negotiating the heavy traffic of the industrial midlands on the way north. We stopped for the night on Bowes moor in Yorkshire but the mist was so thick that the vehicle disappeared as soon as we walked a few paces from it. From behind the blanket of grey came the eerie calls of Curlews, like ghost voices from another existence. The utter loneliness of the place was refreshing after a hard day's motoring.

Next day we made the easy journey to Glasgow where we stopped over with Leslie's friend Charles Palmer. He was a Golden Eagle enthusiast as well as an outstanding bird-photographer, and I spent some blissful hours looking at his fine photographs. That evening he screened his Golden Eagle film for us, a masterpiece which had taken years to complete, after which Leslie showed several of his dealing with Kenya eagles, and then we talked eagles late into the night.

Our road to eagle country lay along Loch Lomond before we turned off onto an abominable rutted track. We explored a likely glen without success, but I was pleased to see a small nesting colony of Common Gulls beside a tarn. While we were driving along in search of a place to spend the night the rain set in, and soon the ruts were running streams. Suddenly a small bird popped out from the side of the road, bobbed its tail, and ran off. It was unmistakably a Common Sandpiper, a species I knew well as a migrant to South Africa. In a trice I was out of the door examining the spot from which it had emerged, and there I found a clutch of three pointed eggs tucked into a tuft of grass and heather. It was a thrilling find for me, if one bears in mind that my only knowledge of the bird had been in its southern winter quarters.

During the night the rain roared on the roof of the van, and at first grey light it was still pouring. After we had breakfasted, Leslie stuck his head out to inspect the weather and pronounced it passable. I protested that we would be drenched in minutes, to which he countered that it was an exceptionally fine day, and if we waited for better conditions we would spend most of the two weeks immured in

26

Leslie Brown at an easily accessible Golden Eagle's eyrie near Loch Lomond.

the vehicle. Being unused to a Scottish summer, I had yet to learn that "passable" weather meant rain which lacked the force to flatten one into the heather.

So we set off into a scudding rain across a raging burn and up a glen; Leslie clad in his kilt led the way while I unashamedly used him as a windbreak. I imagine that we must have looked very much like Good King Wenceslas and his page as the wind blew stronger and I marked his footsteps boldly. Soon I had cause to regret the scorn I had shown for his kilt, for while my long trousers clung soggily to my legs Leslie strode on with his nether regions dry beneath a double layer of tartan. In the occasional periods of reasonable visibility we "spied" the glen for nests, and I saw my first Golden Eagle disappearing into the mist, not unlike that first Black Eagle so many years before. Despite the adverse conditions, we found a new nest site, as well as seeing the nests of a Peregrine Falcon and a Raven. In all we walked about 12 kilometres, during which the only mammal we saw was a sheep dying from pulpy kidney. Leslie explained the importance of this for, although we had seen virtually no natural prey, the eagles are able to subsist to a large extent on dead sheep in certain areas of the Highlands.

The pattern of our days did not vary much as we moved around Argyll in quest of the missing sites. A hearty breakfast would precede a hard day's walking with only a snack for lunch, and in the evening we would hit the fleshpots to replace our depleted calories. After dinner we would take out the map and fill in the new sites we had located that day. These almost always fitted the spatial distribution of pairs that had been predicted when it had been spread out on the floor in London. Quite often Leslie would indicate with uncanny accuracy where he thought we would find nests during the following day's hike. Another point of interest was the frequency with which the eagles used alternate sites, so we always continued our search if the first nest we found showed no signs of being laid in that season. This was to prove useful to me later in Rhodesia, where I never assumed that an eagle was not breeding unless I made a thorough search of the surrounding country. One exceptional case, as will be seen later, was a pair of Martial Eagles which built no fewer than seven different nests in ten years. During our searches we never covered less than eight kilometres in a day, more often it was 16–20 kilometres, and once we had set off into the hills we never encountered a soul. In the course of all this, thanks to Leslie's intimate knowledge of the Highlands, I probably saw more of Golden Eagles than most British ornithologists see in a lifetime.

The more I saw of the Golden Eagle the more I came to compare it with the Black Eagle; indeed it fills much the same ecological niche that the Black Eagle does in Africa. Both species live in mountainous terrain and are exceptionally graceful on the wing, although the Black Eagle undoubtedly takes the honours in this regard. Both rarely call; I never heard the adult Golden Eagles make a sound, and Leslie confirmed that they are not often heard. They each adopt similar hunting methods at times, sneaking along behind a ridge in order to surprise their prey, while capable of spectacular stoops as well. The food of the Golden Eagle is much more varied, for it includes a number of mammals, gamebirds and carrion in its diet, in contrast to the Black Eagle's partiality for dassies; no doubt it would prove disadvantageous

28

A Golden Eagle at its eyrie in Scotland.
(Photograph by Eric Hosking.)

to depend on a single prey species in a climate as rigorous as Scotland's, and carrion has been found to be of particular importance to them in the winter months. Another point of difference is that the Cain and Abel fight does not necessarily have fatal results in the Golden Eagle and it has been estimated that two young survive in about 20% of cases.

As we moved around Argyll, Leslie's ability to find Golden Eagle nests never failed to impress me. Some of these were ridiculously accessible and a child would have been able to walk to them. Others were built on steep crags, but generally even these would have been more easily reached than the nests of Black Eagles which are almost always placed on a substantial cliff. Quite a number of nests we found were very slight structures, which made them even more difficult to locate. Leslie had a special technique which confirmed the existence of such "invisible" sites, but it is a method I may not divulge because of its possible use to egg-collectors, who still harass the Golden Eagle, despite the certainty of prosecution if they are caught.

A fine day in Scotland compensates for all the soakings. On one perfect day we were way up in the hills in the Glen Carron area when Leslie indicated what he thought was the site of an eyrie. On this occasion I felt that he was pushing his luck too far and I bluntly told him so. While we were arguing about the matter, a speck appeared in the sky far above us and then made one of the most spectacular stoops I have ever seen before sweeping up to the very spot that Leslie had indicated. The parent was carrying prey, and a fully grown screaming eaglet emerged into view from the back of a narrow ledge to receive it. I have seldom seen my companion look more pleased with himself than he did at that moment.

After ten years I still remember Scotland with affection, and of a host of recollections several remain more vivid than others. Scenically it is the incredible greeness and the tranquil beauty of the lochs that come to mind. A night on Rannoch moor above Glencoe, when the "Snail" rocked in a shrieking gale, was inexplicably eerie; it was almost as if the cries of the slaughtered Macdonalds still lingered in the air. Of the many new birds I saw the Dipper takes pride of place with its method of feeding under water while walking on the bed of a stream.

The day of parting came all too soon, and Leslie put me on the night train at Inverness while he continued the survey. We were not to meet again for several years, but during those two weeks with him I had learnt a great deal about eagles, and not just the Golden, for we had talked at length about African eagles as well.

4 *Wahlberg's Eagle*

On a day early in April 1896, the excited voices of Africans could be heard approaching a small house perched on top of a steep bank above the Ncema river. Led by Inxnozan, a group of nearly three hundred Matabele warriors burst from the surrounding bush and swept down upon the homestead. It was locked and deserted, but within an hour it was a smouldering ruin, and the horde moved off laughing and joking as they tried on various pieces of plundered apparel.

Sixty-five years later I stood on the spot and recalled the circumstances of this event. All that remained to indicate the position of the house was a crumbling stone outhouse and some terracing. The home was of interest for two reasons: in the first instance, much of it was prefabricated and had been laboriously transported from South Africa to Rhodesia by ox-waggon. Secondly, it had belonged to Frederick Courteney Selous when he had been managing a cattle ranch for Willoughby's Consolidated Company. Renowned as a hunter, Selous had settled at Essexvale to pursue a more peaceful existence. This was of short duration, for when the Matabele rose and began murdering whites, he took his wife to the relative safety of Bulawayo. Ever a man of action, he soon raised a small mounted force which played a distinguished part in suppressing the insurrection. He never returned to rebuild his home, and the grass and bush erased most of the signs of habitation.

Falcon College, where I had come to teach, was within a few kilometres of Selous' ruined homestead. The school lay near the small village of Essexvale in the midst of ranching country where the habitat was mainly acacia thornveld interspersed with other trees, such as marulas and a variety of *Combretum* and *Terminalia* species. One of the things one first notices on arrival in Rhodesia is the profusion of trees, and in ten years I have only managed to learn the names of a fraction of them. The Essexvale area may be described as bushveld, and this helps to explain the term ''going into the bush'' when setting off on a trip away from civilization. The College is a boarding school catering for pupils up to 'A' level, and it has an interesting history. It was established in 1954 on the site of the once prosperous ''Bushtick'' gold mine a few years after it had closed down. In the initial stages the old mine buildings served as classrooms and dormitories, but one of the few relics left now is the brass foot-rail in the tuckshop that once supported the boots of hardened miners as they downed their beer. The College sprawls like a village, and beyond the playing fields may be seen three large minedumps. These are scarred by deep fissures, in the sides of which are the nest holes of White-fronted Bee-eaters and Horus Swifts. Barn Owls live there too, as well as in the yawning mine shafts. As a backdrop to the scene there is a range of humpbacked hills called the Mulungwanes (''knuckles'' in Ndebele) where a number of eagle nests were situated.

A typical nest site of a Wahlberg's Eagle beside a river at Essexvale.

The small nest of a Wahlberg's Eagle with the usual clutch of a single egg.

32

The female Wahlberg's Eagle (behind) returns to take over incubation from the much smaller male.

I stood near the ruins of Selous' homestead with Tim Longden as he indicated a nest in a tree on the steep bank across the river. It belonged to a Wahlberg's Eagle, and was my first Rhodesian eagle's nest which I have referred to as the "Selous" site ever since. It was situated on Longridge Ranch, owned by Tim's parents at the time, and they offered me wonderful hospitality as well as a free run of the ranch. From the top of a steep bank one was level with the nest at a range of 21 metres, and I lost no time in building a hide from which I could observe and photograph.

The eagles had just started to repair the nest at the end of August, not long after their arrival in Rhodesia. This is the very dregs of the year, at the end of the winter months, when the hot weather sets in. The leaves crackle like parchment as the heat intensifies, and the earth is iron-hard under a scorching sun. Corkscrewing into a burnished sky, the ghostly dust-devils spin dry leaves high into the air before allowing them to fall drunkenly back to earth. During September the nest was repaired until the egg was laid at the end of the month. At Essexvale I found this species to be remarkably consistent in its laying time; almost all eggs are laid during the last week of September or first week in October. The eggs are chalky-white with smudges and speckles of red-brown, but they vary enormously from those hardly marked to others which are heavily and attractively blotched. A single egg is the usual clutch, this was invariably the case at Essexvale, but occasionally a clutch of two eggs has been found in southern Africa. In mid-November, after an incubation period of forty-five days, the eaglet hatches.

During this time the days have been growing steadily hotter, until huge thunderheads begin to build up; usually they disperse before returning to mass again while the whole land waits in parched anticipation. Finally, the face of the earth darkens under a crackling leaden sky riven by jags of lightning, the prelude to the drum of rain on the hard ground. The sharp-sweet smell of the first deluge on the dust is a sensation difficult to describe, but a person has only to experience it once to know what I mean. Overnight the earth is released from dusty bondage, and the nuptial flights of termites symbolise the birth of a new year. Green shoots push through, the sticky red puff-ball heads of *Haemanthus* flowers break from the brown earth like a miracle, and the streams flow. This, then, is the world into which the eaglet emerges as it breaks from the shell.

I mentioned earlier the "arrival" of the Selous pair, and this requires explanation. While studying the species in that first year, when I found the majority of the eventual total of eleven nests located within a radius of 16 kilometres of Falcon College, I noticed that they seemed to disappear during April. Thereafter I did not see them again until their sudden appearance at their nests at the end of August. I recorded this phenomenon in print, and found to my surprise that I seemed to have been the first person to draw proper attention to the fact that this species leaves Rhodesia for some five months of the year. Even the standard "Check-List" of Rhodesian birds made no mention of their absence. No one knows where our birds go, but it is assumed that it is somewhere to the north of us. Over the years I have ringed a number of eaglets, but the chances of a long-distance recovery are very slight, and only this will give a clue to the mystery.

A female Wahlberg's Eagle with her seven week old eaglet which is having difficulty in swallowing a large Plated Lizard . . .

. . . so she attempts to pull it out, but the eaglet resists.

35

It is as well to say something more of the adults here. These small brown eagles tend to be unobtrusive, but they are given to making high soaring flights when their clear "klooo-eee" call draws attention to them overhead, often when only just visible to the naked eye. Their coloration varies, and at the Selous site the female was a warm brown in contrast to the chocolate colour of her mate. This distinction also applied at another nest I studied, but it does not appear to be consistent. There is also an interesting creamy-white form of Wahlberg's Eagle; none of these birds occurred at Essexvale, indeed they are rare in all areas, but the one bird I have seen in Rhodesia was a most handsome creature.

The time at which Wahlberg's Eagle breeds is a further point of interest, because it differs from almost all the other southern African eagles. True, the Crowned Eagle usually lays in September or October, but the two species have quite different habitat requirements. The other eagles, with the distinct exception of the Snake Eagles and the Bateleur, lay between April and June in what may be loosely termed the "winter" months. It remains to be satisfactorily explained why this is so, but the answer does not seem to be climatic. A Black Eagle breeding in the south-west Cape will experience heavy rain, while one nesting in the Matopos at the same time will have cool, dry weather. One suggestion is that winter breeding ensures that there is a maximum food supply for the eaglet when it leaves the nest in spring, but I know of no study which has established that there is necessarily an abundance of prey at this time. It's a possible explanation, but it still needs to be backed up by direct evidence. One of the problems with eagles is that people try to make them fit into the same mould as the theories which hold true for sparrows and robins, but they are simply not amenable to such comparisons.

In season, Wahlberg's Eagle is the commonest eagle where it occurs in southern Africa. As mentioned, I located eleven eyries in the Essexvale valley, and there were others I knew of further afield which were not suitable for regular visits. The nests were evenly spaced at about three to six kilometres apart, with a distinct preference for river valleys, although some were sited in flat, open country. The next most common eagle at Essexvale, on the basis of nesting pairs, was the Tawny Eagle, and I knew of three pairs. It is tempting to suggest that Wahlberg's Eagle comes south to nest when it does to utilize a superabundance of prey, moving north again when food becomes short and it is forced into competition with other species. I'm inclined to support the idea that a superabundance of prey is necessary when they have young in the nest, and this is what determines the breeding season. However, to add a further enigmatic touch, they breed in Kenya at precisely the same time as they do in Rhodesia, yet there is a southward migration in Kenya and Tanzania in August-September. The problem of Wahlberg's migration within Africa is, for me, one of the most exciting eagle puzzles left to solve. A friend has even suggested to me, on the evidence of moult pattern, that sub-adult birds may not return to Rhodesia until they are ready to breed. If this is so, where do they spend their years in the wilderness?

The intimate details of their breeding habits are, by comparison, quite uncomplicated. My main study was at the Selous nest, which was watched throughout the breeding

A Wahlberg's Eagle chick hatches.

Three hours later it lies dry but exhausted.

At four days old it begins to look more like an eagle.

37

A female Wahlberg's Eagle broods her small eaglet: an Agama lizard lies in front of her.

On the approach of people she flattens herself in the intruder position.

A female Wahlberg's Eagle stands in a relaxed mood beside her month old eaglet . . .

. . . and a moment later she is all alertness as another bird of prey passes overhead.

cycle in my first year in Rhodesia. Some years later I made further observations at another site and over the years I made numerous visits to the other nests in the vicinity. All in all, it has been possible to build up a comprehensive picture of the home life of this species.

The Selous nest was built up until it was 60 centimetres across, and then the central bowl-shaped depression was lined with green leaves which were added to throughout the incubation period, and for the first month or so of the fledging period. Incubation began as soon as the egg was laid, and I watched the nest for seven days during the incubation period. An interesting point to emerge, in contrast to Leslie Brown's comprehensive study of the species in Kenya, was the substantial part played by

A female Wahlberg's Eagle alights with a lizard clutched in her right foot . . .

. . . then she stands beside her forty-five day old eaglet which has swallowed the lizard whole.

the male in incubation. Previously, males had not been observed to incubate, but the Selous male did so on a number of occasions, and once he sat for nearly two hours. I also recorded a short spell of incubation by a male at another site. The Selous male's periods of incubation usually took the form of nest relief; he would arrive at the nest with prey, and the female would fly off elsewhere to eat it while he settled on the egg. On one occasion he was seen to stand up and turn the egg. When she returned he would make way for her, and once I managed to obtain a photograph of the change-over. I knew that the female was larger than the male, but only when I printed the picture did I realise how small he appeared beside her.

The incubation period is not rewarding for the observer, for there are long periods when nothing at all happens. The longest continuous spell of incubation by the female I watched lasted six hours. The only break in the monotony occurred once when a Fork-tailed Drongo arrived and persistently dive-bombed the incubating male; at first he tolerated it, but then he reacted by snapping at the drongo with his bill. Drongos seem to make it their business to molest birds of prey whenever possible, and not infrequently they follow them back to the nest and harry them there. One drongo at another Wahlberg's nest mobbed a brooding female continuously for seventeen minutes, and at the same time it emitted a perfect imitation of the eagle's own ''kyip, kyip, kyip'' call. So effective was the imitation, that for some while I looked about in vain for the male before realising that the call emanated from the drongo.

As the day of hatching approached, the female became more and more reluctant to leave the nest. Her behaviour when someone approached was to flatten herself onto the nest, a reaction common to all eagles. From below, only the tip of her tail protruding over the nest edge gave her away, and in some species it is impossible to detect the bird on the nest unless one can get level with it. This behaviour has been termed the ''intruder reaction'' and it is also practised by eaglets once they reach a certain age. Sometimes a young eagle just out of the nest will crouch *across* a branch, so that it is obvious to the observer and appears rather ludicrous as it tries to look as inconspicuous as possible. Once a Wahlberg's Eagle on a hatching egg sat so tight that the schoolboy who climbed up was able to put his hand over the nest edge onto the bird's back and catch it. Unfortunately, we did not have a ring with us at the time, so we immediately let it go.

After the rather uninteresting watches during the incubation period, the hatching of the egg came as a welcome event. It first ''pipped'' at about midday, and by 6 p.m. there was a small hole through which the eaglet's beak was visible; the sharp white excrescence, known as the egg-tooth, was clearly visible on the tip of the bill. At one o'clock the next day the eaglet pushed itself free of the egg; by 4 p.m. its down had dried and it lay weakly beside the pieces of egg shell. There were two lizards on the nest when the eaglet emerged, but it was not fed during its first afternoon. The female brooded the eaglet for most of the afternoon, standing up from time to time to inspect it before settling again. She appeared to flick a few small pieces of shell over the nest edge, but no attempt was made to remove the larger portions. Interestingly, the male also brooded the eaglet for twenty minutes, but this was the only time he was seen to do so. When I next observed, the eaglet was five days old, and by this stage the male's sole function was to bring prey to the nest.

A recently hatched Wahlberg's eaglet is covered in dark brown down, and the only other colour is the bright yellow of its legs and cere. Nevertheless, it is an attractive creature, with its dark eyes set in a head too large for its body. As it grows, its down colour lightens to smoky-grey, and by the time it is a month old the feathers are sprouting rapidly through the down. When fully feathered, it is not easily distinguished from the adults. The fledging period is about 70 days, but it may vary by several days either side of this figure.

I weighed and measured the Selous eaglet at weekly intervals, and attempted to

A seven week old Wahlberg's Eagle excercises its wings.

do so for the last time when it was 63 days old. I should have known better. The eaglet flew off the nest to the other side of the river, which was in flood at the time. I had a long walk to find a place where I could cross, and eventually located it lying flat on the ground in an intruder position. As soon as it saw me stalking up, it promptly took off and returned to the opposite bank. I was rather anxious about it, but I need not have worried; that evening it was back on the nest. However, the incident illustrates the caution required by an observer when an eaglet is nearing the time of its departure from the nest. The parents continued to feed their offspring at the nest for a while, but I did not watch the nest for long periods at this stage. I gained the impression that the young eagle probably became independent of the nest after a few weeks, much more rapidly than is the case with larger eagles.

But to return to the beginning of its life, the eaglet was carefully tended by the female during the first fortnight; she was on the nest much of the time while the male's role was to bring food. He usually announced his presence in the area with excited "kyip, kyip, kyip" calls which the female reciprocated, and then he would arrive with prey. The time spent by the parents on the nest declines after two weeks, and with the female off the nest one had to be on constant alert for the male's arrival with food. In contrast to her rather noisy flaps, he landed silently on the nest, and this is a distinction I have noted in several other eagles. When the eaglet was a month old, the male brought prey three times within two and a half hours, during which time the female was not seen at all. I climbed to the nest after his last visit and found that the items brought were a nestling Pied Crow, a Klaas' Cuckoo recently out of the nest and a rat. The birds had been thoroughly plucked, indeed a sparrowhawk could not have made a better job.

However, the above killing rate pales beside the prey received by a month old eaglet at another nest. In one memorable two hours and twenty minutes it was brought ten lizards, the male and female bringing five each. The female brought prey after only five and thirteen minutes away from the nest on two occasions, and the male's shortest intervals between prey delivery were eight and ten minutes. At one stage the male brought a lizard which the eaglet swallowed, and a minute later the female came with another one. Once the eaglet had difficulty in swallowing one of the larger lizards, so the female took the protruding tail in her bill and tried to pull it out; a tug of war ensued, but eventually the eaglet managed to pull the tail free before turning its back on her to gulp it down without further interruption. A feeding rate as rapid as I have described gives the lie to the idea that eagles have difficulty in finding or catching prey, but it must not be imagined that they feed at this rate all the time. The eaglet in this instance was developing rapidly and had a voracious appetite; in contrast it received no food at all during a nine hour watch when it was sixty-four days old.

The food of Wahlberg's Eagle is made up mainly of smaller items, particularly lizards. However, I have found portions of hares on several nests, and it seems likely that they were killed by the eagles themselves. They also prey on birds, particularly young ones recently out of the nest, and once I found a dead Barn Owl in a nest. This eagle is undoubtedly more dashing than generally supposed, and it can stoop in spectacular fashion.

The day to day nest life of this species is now adequately known, and the main problem to solve is that of its migratory movements. I am continuing with my Essexvale census, in its twelfth year as I write, to ascertain details of breeding success. The longer one can maintain such a study, the more meaningful are the eventual results. Every now and again something interesting occurs. In one year, for example, the Selous birds were prevented from breeding when a Giant Eagle Owl took over their nest.

Of similar size to Wahlberg's Eagle is the Long-crested Eagle. It is easily identified by its long, floppy crest, black coloration, white "leggings" and, when it flies, striking white pattern in the wings. However, by comparison with Wahlberg's Eagle it has

A captive first year Long-crested Eagle; its crest is only about half its full length, and it also lacks the yellow eye of the adult.

been poorly studied, and a proper investigation of its breeding biology still needs to be undertaken. In Rhodesia it is generally found in moister well-wooded areas, particularly in the Eastern Districts. It did not occur at Essexvale, so an opportunity to study it at the nest has eluded me. Occasionally, single birds have been seen in the Matopos, and recently one was even reported from the outskirts of Bulawayo. We simply do not know enough at present, but it may be that some birds move around more than was hitherto supposed, for the Long-crested Eagle is generally regarded as a sedentary species. Its breeding season in southern Africa, on the rather limited number of records available, falls between July and December, so it would overlap Wahlberg's Eagle. The two species appear to have a similar diet, and lizards, small mammals and frogs are most often taken by the Long-crested Eagle; it has a very large gape and probably swallows these whole. Most of its hunting is done from a perch, quite often from telegraph poles beside the road, and usually it uses the same perch every day.

I hope that the day is not far off when I will have an opportunity to study the Long-crested Eagle at the nest. With an intimate knowledge of the breeding habits of Wahlberg's Eagle, I shall be interested to see what similarities, and what differences, exist between the two species.

5 *Tawny Eagle*

The Tawny Eagle is common and widely distributed in Africa, and yet, until recently, it has been one of the least studied of our eagles, particularly at the nest. The observations I made at Essexvale over a period of nine years turned out to be the only substantial investigation of breeding biology ever undertaken, but there is still much left to learn. I was fortunate to have studied two nesting pairs to which farm roads gave reasonable access, and later a third pair established themselves in the area.

Few avian reputations have experienced more vicissitudes than that of the Tawny Eagle. When it was named *Aquila rapax*, it must have been considered a rapacious species, but at the nadir of its fortune it was regarded solely as an ignoble carrion-eater. Such varied opinions as "... a powerful and rapacious species ...", "... a not very distinguished bird, that lives on carrion and sneak-thieving ...", "... a dull and unimpressive creature ..." and "... by no means the despicable bird that it is sometimes made out to be ..." have all been expressed.

What, then, is its true character? The answer is that it is made up of a number of facets, and the very key to its success as a species lies in its versatility. It is a scavenger, a pirate and a successful killer of live prey, and in some areas its association with man further enhances its success. Let us now have a closer look at these categories, for this will lead to a better understanding of the species.

The Tawny Eagle's carrion-eating habits do not require much comment, and it associates with vultures and other scavengers such as ravens, crows and Bateleurs at the carcass of a dead animal. There is nothing remarkable in this, but there is much room for research into its inter-relationships with other species at carrion, and this aspect of its behaviour seems to have been neglected. I have seen one feeding on a dead dog beside two White-headed Vultures, apparently in perfect amity. In another instance an observer saw two Tawnies and an immature Bateleur at the corpse of a Red-billed Francolin; they were clearly dominant over the Bateleur, and one Tawny eventually flew off with the francolin. We need a great many more observations of this nature before the behaviour of the Tawny towards other species at carrion can be properly assessed. It will also feed on road casualties, a food supply which is utilized by other scavenging species too. One interesting case of an unusual feeding association describes how a Tawny was perched in a tree above a large male baboon which was eating an unidentified mammal. The eagle watched intently until it departed, and then swooped down and swallowed the tail of the animal which the baboon had discarded.

The piratical habits of the Tawny Eagle follow on logically from its scavenging behaviour, for it seems that its piracy evolved through harrying other species for tit-bits. It has been known to attack birds as small as a Black-shouldered Kite, and

A typical Tawny Eagle's nest which is placed at the very top of a tree.

as large as a Martial Eagle, in attempts to rob them of their prey. A friend of mine lost his trained Lanner Falcon to a Tawny. The Lanner was carrying a dove that it had just killed when the eagle stooped on it and took it in flight. The last he saw of his falcon was when the Tawny disappeared from sight carrying both the Lanner and the dove. There is little doubt that this incident started as an attempt at robbery, but the falcon, taken by surprise, was unable to release its prey in time and was caught too. An incident as spectacular as this gives the lie to the suggestion that the Tawny is ''a dull and unimpressive creature''.

Its tarnished reputation is further redeemed when we consider the quarry it is capable of killing by direct predation. In East Africa it is known to stoop on flamingos and kill them in flight, and in southern Africa it has killed game birds as large as the Black-bellied Korhaan and Crowned Guineafowl; once I saw one make a spectacular stoop at a guineafowl. Tawny Eagles may kill Cattle Egrets too, and one interesting incident took place in the Kafue National Park in Zambia. A Tawny pursued an egret, which twice attempted to take shelter under some Lechwe before it was caught. The eagle flew to a small tree to consume its quarry, but was in turn attacked by a Fish Eagle. The two eagles tumbled through the branches, but eventually the victorious Fish Eagle flew off with the egret and ate it.

One of the problems of recording prey remains at the nest is that it is not always easy to decide what was obtained as carrion and what was directly killed. At my Essexvale nests I gathered 160 prey records over the nine years: birds made up 51,9% of the items, mammals 36,9%, reptiles 10,0% and amphibians 1,2%. I should stress that this represents numbers of prey, and it is possible that by *bulk* mammals may have been more important than birds. Of the birds recorded, half were gamebirds, mostly guineafowl, and I have little doubt that the eagles caught them alive. On the other hand, a Rufous-cheeked Nightjar and a Spotted Eagle Owl were almost certainly road casualties, but it is difficult to know how the Barn Owl I found on a nest was obtained, for I have never known this species to be killed on roads at night. Domestic chickens featured little in my records until one pair moved to a new site, and then I noted nine in two years against a mere two in the six years prior to this. Clearly, they raided an African kraal within their hunting range where chickens roamed freely, and this illustrates that eagles will generally avail themselves of the most easily harvested food source. Hares made up almost half the mammals recorded, but I doubt whether all these were derived as road casualties, certainly the Tawny is quite capable of killing an animal this size. The remains of goat kids, as well as the newly born young of small antelopes, were also seen on nests, but it was always difficult to know if the eagles killed these or found them dead. A portion of an African's dog was undoubtedly dead when found, and I was nearly ill when my nostrils were assailed by the stench as I looked over the nest edge. More than any other eagle I have studied, the hygiene of the Tawny's nest leaves much to be desired. We know little of how this eagle deals with snakes, but one eye-witness account describes how a Tawny swooped down and flew off with a snake. Except for one leguaan, all the reptiles recorded at Essexvale were snakes, and two Puff Adders were amongst those identified.

The Tawny Eagle also benefits from what may be loosely termed its association with man. In areas where more primitive conditions prevail, it scavenges around slaughter-yards and native villages for scraps. This probably occurs seldom, if at all, in southern Africa these days, but at the turn of the century there was a record of a bird shot in a butcher's yard at Potchefstroom in the Transvaal. They are also known to accompany gamebird shoots and carry off wounded birds, but this behaviour seems more prevalent in East Africa, and there appear to be no recent instances of following the gun in South Africa.

The plumages of the Tawny Eagle are even more variable than the aspects of its character, and bird-watchers seeking to identify eagles may, with justification, be confused when confronted with the various guises in which it appears. From my field experience, coupled with an examination of museum specimens, I think that I have at last obtained a reasonably clear idea of plumages. Young birds leave the nest with a uniform pale red-brown plumage. With the passage of time, their feathers abrade and bleach until they are almost creamy-white, and quite often they retain some reddish feathering on the head and neck, where presumably the least wear takes place. My friend Alan Kemp has coined the term "blondes" for these pale birds, and it is especially apposite because particularly white birds could then be called peroxide blondes. The first moult does not occur until the immatures are over a year out of the nest, but at present we do not know precisely when and, in any case, it is a gradual process. Their next plumage is tawny, and first streaking appears on the sides of the breast. At the next moult there is an intensification of the dark-brown streaking of the breast, which also develops on the wing converts and on the back. The final moult sees a deeper tawny colour, and the streaking becomes heavier still. I estimate that it takes four years to reach this adult state, and the brown iris of the sub-adult bird changes to yellow between the second and third year. I should stress here that my remarks apply to southern African birds.

However, just to add confusion to the situation, some male birds assume a uniform buff plumage which they retain without the development of streaking. The pair that I studied most closely were so different in coloration that an unskilled observer, not seeing them together at the nest, could be forgiven for thinking that they were two different species of eagles. The photographs illustrating this chapter show this pair well, and they retained their respective plumages over the years without change. I had thought, on the strength of this pair, that there was a consistent plumage difference between the sexes, but museum specimens revealed that dark streaky males existed too. It seems, though, that males are never as heavily streaked as females, and this generalization applies to a number of other species of "streaked" eagles as well, the African Hawk-Eagle being a good example.

Then, to add even further complication to the problem of identification, there is an influx of migrant eagles at the beginning of the rains which, in the areas of summer rainfall where they occur, means from about the beginning of November. These migrants are particularly common in Rhodesia, but they are also found in the Transvaal, Botswana, Natal and South West Africa. However, they have only been properly studied in Rhodesia, and my remarks must be taken to apply to this area.

A dark, streaky Tawny Eagle with her three week old eaglet.

Her mate was a much paler bird with a handsome buffy plumage.

51

A dark, streaky Tawny Eagle, probably a female.

Two species are involved, the Steppe Eagle and the Lesser Spotted Eagle. The former ranges from south-western Russia to Mongolia, while the latter is found mainly in central Europe, extending as far east as western Russia. A comprehensive guide to the identification of these two "big brown jobs" would involve undue complexity here, but briefly the Steppe Eagle is similar in general appearance and size to the Tawny, while the Lesser Spotted Eagle is closer to Wahlberg's Eagle in size. One of the most useful methods of separation, in my experience, is to look at the "leggings". The Steppe has baggy trousers, while the Lesser Spotted has "stovepipes". For all practical purposes, however, the most useful guide to the fact that one is seeing migrant eagles is that they occur in flocks, while the resident species do not. In mixed flocks Steppe Eagles appear to outnumber the Lesser Spotted Eagles, and the latter are more likely to be found singly.

An unusual aspect of their stay with us is their diet, which is principally termite alates. On occasions, mixed flocks of more than a hundred of these eagles may be seen feeding on the ground on winged termites emerging from their nests. It is a ludicrous sight to see these large eagles running around, like so many ungainly chickens, in pursuit of their minuscule quarry. They will also attend quelea colonies, so that during their stay in southern Africa they harvest a superabundant food supply which is quite different from what they eat in Europe and Russia. There are a number of other fascinating aspects which have only recently been revealed, but one of the most interesting is that, on present evidence, it seems that only sub-adult Steppe Eagles come to southern Africa to winter, while adult birds stop off in East Africa. It has been suggested that this spreads the load of competition within the species, and it will be a remarkable phenomenon if it can be fully demonstrated. Another interesting feature is that, while the migrant eagles come south to Rhodesia in November where they follow the rain fronts, they do not move north again by the same route, and most of them disappear by the end of December. Where do they go when they leave Rhodesia, and by what route do they return north?

The Tawny Eagle's nest is one of the most characteristic of all the African eagles, and is placed on top of a tree so that it is open to the sky. The platform of sticks is usually about a metre across, but it does not normally achieve the bulk of other eagle nests. This is because a site is not usually occupied for any length of time, since they tend to move their nests more than any other eagles except the Snake Eagles. I have sought a reason for this, and think that I may have found at least a partial answer. Although they use a variety of trees in which to breed, they seem to prefer flat-topped thorn trees. I noticed that nests were generally abandoned when the surrounding branches on the crown of the tree grew up and apparently obstructed free access to the nest, but a further reason may be that once nests achieve a certain weight they can no longer be supported by the smaller branches of the tree's crown. The longest consecutive period that a nest was used at Essexvale was three years. The distance of a move to a new site varied, but generally it was not very far; the shortest move was only 30 metres. Over a period of nine years one pair had three nest sites (they did not breed in one year) and another four. Another pair, located towards the end of the study, used a nest twice running.

The female Tawny Eagle alights while the male is feeding the eaglet.

The pale male on the left and the dark female frame their three week old eaglet.

54

*The male takes off onto the breeze
. . .*

*. . . leaving the female to guard
the eaglet.*

55

The centre of the nest is lined either with greenery, or dry material, or both. The Tawny tends to use dry material and miscellaneous scraps, a feature I have not noted in other eagles I have studied. Some of the more unusual items recorded were a large empty polythene bag, newspaper, seed pods, brown paper and the cover of a schoolboy's exercise book. The clutch of two eggs is laid between April and June, but with a definite May peak in Rhodesia, the only area for which many nest records exist. The eggs are chalky-white, usually with some red markings, but in my experience they are never heavily marked.

I have not been able to establish the exact incubation period. On the one occasion that I spent a great deal of effort to get an accurate laying date for the first egg it failed to hatch. Of course, in the perverse way Fortune deals in these matters, the second egg did, but then I did not know how long after the first it was laid. At all events, I established that incubation took between 42–44 days on one occasion, and not less than 44 and not more than 47 days in another instance. It seems probable that incubation takes close on 44 days. No long watches were undertaken during the incubation period, but a great many visits were made to nests over the nine years. At no time was a male flushed from a nest, and the circumstantial evidence suggests that the female does almost all the incubation.

The young hatch at least two days apart, and a Cain and Abel battle takes place. However, its outcome is not as relentlessly invariable as that of the Black Eagle, and I know of three authentic cases in southern Africa where two young were successfully reared. At Essexvale only the older eaglets survived, and I have witnessed the struggle on two occasions. Once I successfully reared an eaglet which was rescued before it was seriously injured, and I eventually released it into the wild. The last I heard of it, some weeks later, was an irate report by an African that a screeching eagle had swooped down on him on a lonely road and caused him to leap for his life from his bicycle. I could only hope that it would soon develop a fear of humans, for such behaviour was not calculated to lead to longevity.

The eaglet develops rapidly, first feathers appear on the back at three weeks and substantially cover the upperparts by the time it is five weeks old. I shall deal with this aspect of rapid feather development in more detail when I come to the Snake Eagles, but it seems to be an adaption developed by several raptorial species which have nests exposed to the elements. Once the young bird has this covering it can be left unattended on the nest, and both parents are free to hunt. Apart from the Tawny Eagle and Snake Eagles, this rapid feather development is found in the Secretary Bird, the Bateleur and the vultures.

The limited watches I made from a hide during the fledging period established that the female broods the eaglet closely for the first week or so, but then she may leave it unattended for fairly long periods, even while it is still downy. Once a thirteen day old eaglet, which had a bulging crop, was left alone on the nest for two and a half hours. It suffered no apparent discomfort, and the female remained on a favourite perch from which she could watch the nest. In the early stages the male brought most of the prey to the nest, and when the eaglet was three weeks old he arrived while the female was absent. Although initially hesitant, he eventually tore up the prey and fed the chick continuously for ten minutes until his mate returned. This was a red letter day for me, because it was one of the few occasions when I have seen a male bird of prey feed a chick. The parents remained together on the nest for a few minutes, but exchanged no calls. Indeed, in all the time I have studied the Tawny, I have yet to hear the adults make any call. The female is reported to emit a sibilant "shreep-shreep" at the nest, and a barking "kowk-kowk" call is made by soaring birds, probably in display. For me they have maintained a sphinx-like silence, and only the eaglet has obliged me with a squealing "wee-yik, wee-yik" hunger call when the parents were approaching with food.

With the parents away from the nest for long periods, one's entertainment depends on the eaglet, and there is no lack of interest. The eaglet was seen to stand briefly at 22 days, and next day it stood with more confidence to eject a white jet of excreta over the nest edge. This is a vital function, for the nest would otherwise become intolerably fouled; even very small eaglets instinctively aim for the edge, even if they don't quite make it at times. When a month old it could walk around the nest, but its demeanour was cautious, and it leant well forward to maintain its balance. After such bouts of activity it would sometimes lie down on its side, one leg stretched out, and doze off. The foot would be held loosely open and occasionally the talons would twitch – I could almost imagine it dreaming of a nice piece of mature carrion! When I next watched at 39 days, the eaglet was seen to feed itself. The male brought in a Wattled Plover which the eaglet snatched from him and mantled over. This mantling behaviour, once the young bird reaches a certain age, is instinctive; one supposes that it has evolved in order to hide the prey from potential robbers, so its reaction to its own parent is the same as it would be to any other bird of prey. Once the male had left, it tore up the plover, and the only difficulty it had was in gulping down the long yellow legs.

We ringed the eaglet that day, and when the climber's head appeared over the nest edge it reacted with typical threat behaviour: the feathers on its neck and back were raised, gape opened wide, wings held out and slapping blows delivered with the wings. I have observed this behaviour in a number of other eagles in similar circumstances, and when one attempts to handle them for ringing they lean well back and use their claws to advantage, thus there is a further reason for not ringing eaglets too late in the fledging period. Individual birds vary in their reaction; some will maintain an intruder position until actually handled, while others will adopt threatening behaviour as soon as a head appears over the nest edge. Possibly the generally docile behaviour of young Black Eagles results from the fact that the intruder usually appears by rope from above, which places them at a distinct disadvantage.

First vigorous wing flapping was noted when the eaglet was seven weeks old, but my hand-reared eaglet made some clumsy attempts when a month old. Apart from these wing exercises, there is little activity during the latter part of the fledging period, and one is lucky to be in the hide when prey is brought in. The feathered eaglet spent much of its time preening and sleeping; occasionally it nibbled the nest sticks or "attacked" a bone in the nest with its talons. Sometimes it stood for long periods peering intently at a flock of guineafowl far below. And so its days drew on, until one day it spread its wings on the breeze and made its first flight. I recorded the fledging period on seven occasions, and it lay between eleven and twelve weeks.

The young eagle, once fledged, does not abandon the nest; it still receives food from its parents there, rests on it during the day and uses it as a roost at night. In one year an eaglet remained attached to a nest for six weeks after its first flight, and then ranged further afield before disappearing from the nest area. I have had a recovery of one of my ringed eaglets which left the nest at the end of September and was shot 48 kilometres NNE of its nest site two years later, apparently because it was taking domestic chickens.

I shall always retain vivid memories of the Tawny Eagle, particularly the pair I photographed that one year. Their nest was near the top of an isolated hill in open grassland, and my hide was perched in a tree at the same level with it. The flaxen grass, interspersed with patches of bare red earth and contour ridges, lay far below me, like an abstract design executed in pastels on an immense sun-washed canvas. As I sat in the hide I would hear the faint swish of a breeze sifted through pinions, and a moment later the female arrived, huge talons stretched forward and wings thrown back in an alighting instant. The picture was complete.

A female Tawny Eagle alights at her nest with a chicken.

The ''stovepipe'' leggings of this migratory Lesser Spotted Eagle are a useful aid to identification.

An immature migrant Steppe Eagle on the ground after termites, the main food of this species in southern Africa.

60

A recently fledged Tawny Eagle in fresh reddish plumage.

A Tawny Eagle in worn white plumage before its first moult: some reddish feathers still remain on the face.

61

6 *The Crowned Eagle at Home*

Of all the African eagles, the Crowned is considered by many to be the most spectacular. Its striking appearance can not fail to impress, and, although not the largest of our eagles in respect of wing-span, it is probably the most powerful.

The Crowned Eagle resembles a huge goshawk, with its short, broad wings and long tail, both of which are heavily barred. For a bird of its size it is remarkably agile and manoeuvrable, and a friend described to me how one snatched a monkey in a tree from below before any member of the troop had time to give the alarm.

The Crowned Eagle is primarily a forest dweller, an environment to which it is adapted, where it may easily be overlooked during a short visit to its habitat. But if one spends any length of time in an area where a pair occurs, then they will reveal their presence. This is because they are noisy birds and will call frequently, especially at the nest. In addition, they perform an undulating display flight above the forest during which they call, the male at a higher pitch than the female. The purpose of this is to advertise their territory, something which would be difficult to do if they remained beneath the forest canopy. Some people will be familiar with the territorial display of another forest raptor, the African Goshawk, which advertises its presence by flying at a great height emitting a metallic clicking note.

Although it was long thought that monkeys made up a large proportion of the dict of this species, recent findings indicate that they do not often prey on them. In Kenya, it has been estimated that monkeys do not comprise more than 10% of their diet. One of their favourite items of prey is the small forest antelope, the Suni, but in the Matopos they feed mainly on dassies. The Crowned Eagle is particularly well suited to capturing forest prey, and usually "still hunts" by perching on a branch waiting for prey to pass below. Its mottled underparts blend with the dappled light and shade beneath the tree's canopy, and it is difficult to detect. After having crushed the life out of its victim with its enormous feet – the most powerful eagle talons in Africa – it is able to make a vertical take-off with its prey to a branch above. When the prey is too heavy to lift, it has been known to eat some of it first, and then cache the remainder if there is a surplus over its immediate requirements.

In Kenya, Leslie Brown watched a male Sykes' Monkey that deliberately baited a Crowned Eagle by rushing up a tree and snatching at the feet of the perched eagle. On other occasions, when the eagle was brooding a small eaglet, the monkey bounded all round her, sometimes landing on the nest, and even jumping over her back several times. The eagle threatened him, even grasping with her talons at her tormentor, but the monkey was too agile. A description of this behaviour may be found in *The Ibis* and it must rank as one of the most entertaining articles ever to appear in that journal.

A female Crowned Eagle at her nest in the Matopos.

The female Crowned Eagle throws forward her massive talons as she alights.

Before moving to Rhodesia, I had never seen a Crowned Eagle in the wild, although I had been shown two massive nests of this species near Grahamstown. I remember glimpsing my first one in thick forest above Umtali in the Eastern Districts of Rhodesia, and I recall that my most vivid impression when it flew was of the barring and striking chestnut underwing coverts. I entertained little hope of photographing this species at the nest because, as far as I knew, it did not occur within reasonable striking distance of Essexvale; thus it was with alacrity that I accepted my friend Carl Vernon's invitation to visit a probable nest site in the Matopos. At that time the situation with regard to the Crowned Eagle in the Matopos was rather vague; they were known to occur, but were considered rare. Over the years, as a result of increased exploration in search of Black Eagles, it has been found that they are quite widely distributed, and several breeding pairs have been located. The Matopos can by no means be called a forest area, although heavily timbered in parts, but the Crowned Eagles find it suitable. They prey almost entirely on dassies, and with the Black and African Hawk-Eagle make up a trio of eagles known to harvest this rich food source. Nor are they the only predators of the dassie, which must also contend with predatory mammals, and snakes such as the Black Mamba and Python. In the National Park area of the Matopos the ''balance of nature'' prevails, but in neighbouring Tribal Trust land, where Africans hunt dassies relentlessly, while their cattle compete with them for food, there is a serious decline in the dassie population. Although the evidence is not conclusive at present, it appears that a number of Black Eagles in Tribal Trust land are not breeding successfully, and it would appear that the food-chain has been seriously affected by man.

The eyrie visited by Carl and myself early in 1962 lay in a remote valley nearly 100 kilometres from Bulawayo where it was situated in a large tree on the side of a hill strewn with huge boulders. We hoped to find a fully grown eaglet on the nest, or at least signs that one had recently been reared. The nest looked big from below, but only when we had climbed level with it did I realise how vast it was, for a man could have lain full length on top of it. It did not seem to have been recently used, but there appeared to be a few bones in the centre of the nest, so I decided to climb the tree. The main trunk gave little purchase, and I had to bear-hug my way up towards the first branches with a progress as gradual as it was exhausting. When I was about four metres from the base of the tree, I felt a tingling sensation under the palm of my hand, and suddenly the full horror of realization dawned on me – I had put my hand over the entrance of a wild bees' nest! As I withdrew it, they poured out to attack, and I slid some of the way down the trunk before falling onto a boulder. Fortunately Carl called out from beneath the tree to ask what had happened, and my tormentors made, if I may be excused the term, a bee-line for him. Relieved of immediate assault, I hobbled away as fast as I could.

Some while later we met in the valley below, where I thanked Carl for unwittingly providing relief as we scraped stings from each other. I suppose it could have been worse, for wild Rhodesian bees are notoriously vicious, and several unfortunate people have been stung to death by them. My knee had taken a hard knock in the fall, and was by now very painful; all I wanted to do was go home, but then I remembered that I had left my camera at the base of the tree. I limped back up the slope. By then the bees had composed themselves, so my stealthy approach did not disturb them. This was just as well, for I would have been quite unable to run away.

In November of that same year, accompanied by Carl and some of my pupils, I returned to the nest, and we were delighted to find that it contained a downy eaglet about a week old. We set up my portable hide on the slope level with the nest, and at 9 a.m. they left me to try my luck. I did not have long to wait before I saw the female approaching, and I just had time to apply my eye to the viewfinder to see a blur of barred wings as I pressed the shutter, which was set at 1/1000th of a second. Although this did not freeze her completely, I was later thrilled to find

The female Crowned Eagle calls loudly as people approach the nest: her huge feet rest on a branch as thick as a man's thigh.

The female Crowned Eagle returns to the nest with a spray of green nest lining.

the impression of power I had captured as she threw forward her massive talons just prior to landing. The branch behind the nest was scarred by her claws and, despite the fact that it was as thick as a man's thigh, her talons wrapped round over the top of it. A large branch across the front of the nest prevented a full view of her, but later she jumped onto the nest and moved forward to brood the eaglet. I'm always fascinated by the care with which eagles place their feet at such times, and caution is very necessary when one considers that a foot dwarfs a small eaglet that could easily be injured if trodden upon. After a while she was settled to her satisfaction, and little of interest occurred until a pair of Yellow-throated Sparrows landed on the edge of the nest. They were intent on gathering some stray pieces

The male Crowned Eagle alights with prey while the female screams loudly.

of the eagle's down with which to line their own nest. The female peered intently at them, cocking her head to one side, but the diminutive sparrows, no longer than her bill, went about their task undeterred.

As nothing further happened after the departure of the sparrows, I turned my attention to the various lizards which had come out to warm themselves on the rock in front of the hide. Except for the Namib desert, I know of no area in southern Africa that can match the variety of lizards found in the Matopos. They come in all shapes and colours, and often their coloration blends with the lichens on the rocks. One fat Agama lizard I saw that day was as imaginatively coloured as a child's painting for its ridged head was bright powder-blue, followed by a grey body and an orange tail; add to this its tiny beady eyes and grinning slit of a mouth, and you could not wish for a more entertaining creature. My studies of the lizards were cut short by excited calling from the female eagle, and at that moment the male arrived at the nest. He came so suddenly and quietly, that I was unable to see whether he had prey. However, as the eaglet was not subsequently fed, he had probably brought nothing. He remained for only a minute or two, long enough for me to see how much smaller than the female he was, and I noted too that his breast was not as heavily blotched as hers. Not long afterwards I heard the others coming up to fetch me, whereupon the female moved to the branch behind the nest and called loudly until they were right below the nest tree. She was certainly one of the boldest and most imposing eagles I had seen, and I hoped very much to renew her acquaintance.

Having snatched the prey, the female turns her back on him and mantles over it.

This came about in November a year later, when there was again a small downy eaglet in the nest. This time we camped in the valley below, and I left my hide in place that afternoon. She was incredibly vocal that evening, calling frequently until it was almost dark. Next morning, before sunrise, she was calling again, while I lay in my sleeping-bag and watched her with binoculars. After a hurried breakfast, I was installed in the hide at 6.30 a.m., the earliest I have ever started eagle photography. Fortune now made full atonement for the incident with the bees, for the branch obscuring the nest had fallen down. Much of the old nest had collapsed too, and the new structure was considerably smaller. The sun was scarcely on the nest when the female arrived with a spray of green leaves in her bill; she dropped this on the nest and then fussed about arranging some sticks before settling down to brood. At eight o'clock she stood up in a hunched position and called as the male arrived with a dassie. She snatched this, turned her back on him, and mantled over it while he looked on for a few moments before leaving. The Crowned Eagle is the only eagle in my experience where the female mantles so aggressively in the presence of the male, and I noted similar behaviour at another nest.

She abandoned her mantling posture soon after the male's departure and started to feed the eaglet, a process which lasted for ten minutes. I noticed that it was fed mostly on pieces of liver, and I had the impression that this Promeathean meal was intentionally selected for it by the female. On completion of the feed, she stood over the eaglet shading it, and little of note occurred until the male made a brief visit without prey. She immediately flung her mantling ''umbrella'' over the dassie and maintained this position until he departed. Later a troop of baboons passed close behind the hide, and I imagine that there would have been panic had I emerged.

There followed a lapse of four years before I carried out observations at a Crowned Eagle's nest again, and the site was on a wooded slope above a dam in the Matopos. This structure was even larger than the one previously described, being just over two metres across the top. It seemed remarkable to me that the eagles nested there at all, for the nest was visible from a popular picnic spot below. At the beginning of November there was a three week old eaglet on the nest, although there had been two eggs originally. Once again two eggs are laid, but the smaller eaglet is killed for there is no record of a Crowned rearing two young. By backing off up the slope I was again able to place my portable hide in a position level with the nest. I observed for a morning during this first visit, but little of interest took place.

I watched for another morning when the eaglet was five weeks old, and this time there was more activity. The female landed in the nest tree in complete silence, and I only noticed her because a male Paradise Flycatcher made persistent dive-bombing attacks, even striking her a number of times. I have mentioned that most female eagles may be heard when they land at the nest, and the female Crowned Eagle's ability to fly silently, despite her size, must be advantageous in a stealthy attack on prey. The flycatcher's attacks eventually elicited a response when she opened her gape at him and raised her impressive crest. Eventually he departed and she jumped onto the nest to stand beside the eaglet. After a while she decided on some nest renovation, and for fully five minutes she prodded, pulled, dug and rearranged,

A female Crowned Eagle with her five week old eaglet on their huge nest.

The female Crowned Eagle perched above her nest: her breast markings blend well with the leaves.

The ten week old Crowned Eagle stretches its wings . . .

. . . and then backs to the edge of the nest to defecate.

73

while the eaglet watched the proceedings. While all this was going on a Yellow-throated Sparrow appeared to fetch some down for its nest, just as I had seen one do all those years before. When she had finished the eaglet stood up weakly to defecate, after which it attempted some abortive wing flaps that resulted in a ludicrous collapse onto its face.

At 9.50 a.m. the female called loudly and the male alighted with a dassie; her mantling behaviour was identical to that previously described. When he left she fed the eaglet which also tried, unsuccessfully, to pull off pieces itself. Once she withdrew a difficult piece from its mouth and tore it in half before offering it again. She swallowed a large awkward piece herself and got into such contortions over it that for a while I thought she would choke. The entire meal, during which she consumed a fair amount herself, lasted for forty minutes, and on its completion the gorged eaglet dozed off while she stood over it. All was peace until she somehow managed to get her hind claw jammed amongst the nest sticks, and she did a jig for several seconds before wrenching it free.

I next visited the nest when the eaglet was ten weeks old, and in the interim it had grown into a handsome creature with immaculate white head, legs and underparts, offset against the barred tail and grey back which had white edges to the feathers. Superficially it is not unlike the young Martial Eagle, but the long barred tail, barred underwings and lack of grey on the head would serve to distinguish it. A short spell of two hours in the hide produced little notable activity, and the eaglet either lay down and rested, or preened, or wandered about the nest. There was no prey visible and I did not see the parents until they flew high overhead just as I was leaving.

The fledging period varies between 103 and 115 days in five cases recorded in Kenya by Leslie Brown, but what is of extreme interest is the duration of the post-fledging period there. He found that young birds were still fed by their parents for 270–350 days after their first flight, and this resulted in a breeding cycle of over 500 days, so that they usually breed once every two years. He has suggested that this protracted period of dependence results in a young eagle which is more likely to survive to maturity. While this may apply in Kenya, it is not necessarily the case in southern Africa, for my friend Terry Oatley has kept a record of breeding at a nest near Pieter-maritzburg in Natal. Here the Crowned Eagles have bred regularly each year, and it was known that the young eagle survived after fledging on at least two occasions, because the parents have had to chase it away prior to breeding the following year.

Thus the Crowned Eagle, which has been studied more intensively than any other eagle in the world, reveals a different breeding rhythm, apparently, in two separate areas. In eagle studies comparisons are never odious, and one should never hold back from a study for fear of repetition – whatever the outcome the findings will still prove valuable.

7 *Magnificent Martial*

My almost fanatical admiration of the Martial Eagle developed long before I had ever seen one. While still at school, I had acquired a copy of "Knight in Africa" by Capt. C.W.R. Knight, and in this book he gave a fascinating account of two trips to South Africa in quest of eagles in the early nineteen-thirties. His first visit had been in the nature of a reconnaissance, in the course of which he had located an unoccupied Martial's nest which was suitable for photography. On returning from a lecture tour of the United States with Mr. Ramshaw, his famous trained Golden Eagle, he found a telegram from a friend in South Africa awaiting him at his home in Kent which merely said, "EGG LAID". He took the next available ship to Cape Town, trekked into the interior, and obtained a remarkable series of pictures that sent me into raptures when I first saw the book; I felt that the Martial was quite a bird to have lured a man all that way on the off chance of obtaining photographs of it.

Unfortunately, the Martial Eagle has been widely persecuted in South Africa, where it is now rare or extinct in settled areas, and my chances of seeing it in the south-west Cape were indeed remote. It was not until I was taken on a visit to the Kruger National Park that I saw one, and it fulfilled all my expectations. It sat high up in a gnarled dead tree intently surveying the distant bushveld, and I felt that *bellicosus* was as suitable a scientific name as has ever been given to an eagle. Although it did not clasp a crag with crooked hands, it certainly stood "ring'd with the azure world", and the scene could not have been bettered. I even managed to obtain a picture which, although by no means a striking portrait, still conveys to me the essence of that magnificent creature. Since that first occasion I have seen the Martial in many places: soaring over a wooded kloof high in the foothills of the Drakensberg; sailing across the sweeping immensity of the Namib desert; flying above the savannas of Rhodesia and Botswana; yet whatever the scene, it has never failed to impart a touch of grandeur by its presence.

When I first viewed the Essexvale valley from the hills above it, I little realised that I was within a kilometre of a Martial's nest. I located it almost a year later on information from a local farmer who had given me rough directions, and once in the right area I spotted the eyrie from a long way off, for it stood out starkly in the upper branches of an African Beech growing on a sparsely wooded hillside. The massive nest was only six metres above the ground in a tree that looked almost too spindly to support it, but the site afforded the birds a panoramic view of the surrounding country. Also, there were good air currents on the hill slope, a factor which I found to be important in their selection of subsequent nest sites over the years.

My first Martial Eagle surveyed the surrounding bushveld from this gnarled tree in the Kruger National Park.

A Martial Eagle's eyrie at Essexvale, the first site at which I took photographs.

It is generally stated that the Martial remains attached to one nest, perhaps with an alternate site, but the Essexvale pair nearly drove me to distraction with the capricious way in which they constructed new nests, or unexpectedly returned to old ones. It seemed to make no difference whether they reared an eaglet successfully, or failed, or missed a year's breeding; they never used the same site consecutively, and in the ten years 1962–1971 I located no fewer than seven different nests over an area of 260 hectares. It may sound a simple task to track these down in an area this size, but the hills were pleated with a mass of small valleys and a lot of hard searching was necessary. However, I found that most nests were situated in the neck of a valley, where air currents apparently suited them, and this assisted my task. In the

77

six years in which they were known to breed they raised three young, but they may have reared others in nests which I only found at a later stage.

I photographed and made observations in 1962, 1964 and 1969 at three different nests, but only once was it necessary to build a hide in a tree to get level with the nest, and at the other two sites I merely had to erect my portable ground hide on the steep slope overlooking them. The 1962 eyrie was first found in mid-June when it was well lined with green leaves, and a month later it contained a chalky-white egg which was lightly marked with a few reddish blotches. The female lay so flat in the nest that it was not possible to see her from a position level with the nest, and she only flew when I was half way up the tree.

During the incubation period I watched the nest for six hours, which was made up of short spells on three different afternoons. Only the female was seen to incubate on these occasions, when she sat stolidly for much of the time. One afternoon she called to the male for ten minutes, and they exchanged soft musical "quolp" and "kloo-ee" notes. Although never remotely approaching the impressive volume of the Crowned Eagle, their calls were pleasant when heard at close quarters. Eventually she left the nest and remained away for just over half an hour, and I have little doubt that the male had brought prey for her. On another occasion she returned soon after I was installed in the hide and flew off with the mongoose that had been lying on the nest. She alighted in a tree across the valley and ate it, while I watched the whole meal with binoculars through a peep-hole in the side of the hide. Once the mongoose was consumed, she cleaned each of her massive claws in turn before vigorously rubbing both sides of her bill against a rough vertical branch. Then, her toilet complete, she returned to resume the task of incubation.

The egg must have been very near to hatching, for when I returned three weeks later after a photographic trip to Game Reserves in Mozambique and Zambia, I found a downy eaglet which was close on three weeks old. It was an attractive "two-tone" creature, grey above and white below, and it did not lack for food: beside it lay the remains of three domestic chickens and a Coqui Francolin, and some feathers indicated that a guineafowl had been on the menu too within the last few days.

Two days later I was able to take some time off during the afternoon, and spent a rewarding hour in the hide. The female returned to the nest, picked up a chicken's carcass in her bill, and flew off with it. As she glided away she swung her feet forwards and transferred the prey to her claws in one graceful movement. I heard her somewhere behind the hide making soft clucking noises, not unlike those of a hen, and shortly after this the male landed on the nest. He removed a Coqui Francolin in his bill, and as he swept away he transferred it to his claws just as the female had done. A while later the female returned, followed shortly by the male, and I was able to obtain a picture as they framed the eaglet between them. The female was a much bulkier bird, and her mate, with his slighter build and less relaxed stance, gave the impression of a giant goshawk. He remained for several minutes, and on his departure the female started to feed the eaglet on an unidentified bird which she fetched from the back of the nest. Not long after this I was collected from the hide, and she flew off with a leg of the bird in her bill. This must have been swallowed

78

A three week old Martial Eagle chick: the birds lying in front of it are a Coqui Francolin and two chickens.

First feathers appear at five weeks: a hare lies behind the eaglet.

By eight weeks the eaglet is well feathered.

79

or dropped, for as we were leaving she glided past with a large spray of green leaves in her bill. I was well pleased with that hour's photography, for I had obtained several alighting pictures as well as the portrait of the pair on their huge nest.

I put in a few more hours in the hide when the eaglet was four and five weeks old, but I obtained no more pictures of the adults that year. The eaglet grew rapidly; at five weeks old feathers were breaking through the down on its back, and three weeks later it was almost completely feathered. It fledged when approximately a hundred days old, a handsome young eagle with snowy white underparts and grey above. Its dark eyes were set beneath a prominent "eyebrow", and with its slight crest it possesses one of the finest of all eagle heads.

The 1964 site was also in an African Beech at a height of six metres, but this time the tree grew on a particularly steep slope in the neck of a narrow valley. There was an egg when I found it at the end of May, the eaglet hatched in mid-June, and my first session in the hide was when it was a week old. The female returned bringing green leaves, a not uncommon occurrence with eagles when they have been disturbed from the nest, and possibly a form of "displacement activity". She merely dumped the leaves on the nest, and then proceeded to feed herself and the eaglet on a hare. Shortly after midday the male, his crop bulging from a good feed, came to the nest with the rear half of a guineafowl which he deposited. The female took this up in her bill and flew off with it while he remained behind. He seemed ill at ease initially, but eventually he settled to brood the eaglet. He stood up and resettled a number of times, perservering in his task for fifteen minutes. When the female perched in a tree behind the hide he stood up, and a little while later departed; one almost had the impression that he was pleased to go. Indeed, it is one of the few instances in my experience where a male has brooded an eaglet. The female returned shortly afterwards and stood shading the eaglet for the next hour, then she fed it some more hare before being disturbed by my relief party, who brought news of having found an old Martial's nest in another valley. This site, as it turned out, was to be renovated and used the following year. During a couple of hours' observation a week later, the pattern of parental behaviour was much the same. The female remained on the nest shading the eaglet and again, just after midday, the male paid a visit with prey, in this case a mongoose.

I did not visit the nest again until the eaglet was seventy-five days old. I had Leslie Brown with me, and when I tried to climb the tree to ring the eaglet it stood up and flapped away to land on the opposite side of the valley. I was surprised that it could fly so well and left after so little hesitation; there seems little doubt that it would have fledged naturally well before the 100 days recorded for the 1962 eaglet. Leslie had noted precisely where it landed, and after a long walk round the head of the valley we came upon it lying flat in the grass. I ringed it, and then picked it up for a closer examination. As I held the eaglet on its side to inspect the underside of its tail, it suddenly pulled a leg free and struck me full in the face with an open foot. Fortunately for me, it immediately released its grip, but not before it had given me the fright of my life. We placed it in a tree, and then retired quietly to examine the damage. The front claw had made a small hole above one eye, the

A Martial Eagle just out of the nest: the grey feathers on the head distinguish it from the young Crowned Eagle.

The adult Martial Eagles, the male on the right, frame a downy eaglet on their huge nest.

While the male looks on, the female Martial Eagle leaves the nest with the remains of a gamebird in her bill.

hind claw had curled in under my upper lip, and the other two claws had straddled my face. I shudder to think what might have happened had it held on and exerted pressure, or if it had stuck a claw in my eye.

This experience had an interesting sequel. The young eagle had been ringed on 26th August 1964, and on 29th June the following year it was "recovered" (almost certainly a euphemism for shot) some 65 kilometres north-west of its nest site. This illustrated not only that its early fledging resulted in no harm, but also that juveniles wander away from the nest area; in this instance it was well out of the way by the time the adults bred the following year.

The 1965 eaglet disappeared from the nest without trace between its second and third week, one of those inexplicable events which one has to accept philosophically

The female Martial Eagle alights at the nest . . .

in the circumstances. It had been possible to ascertain that the incubation period lay between 44 and 51 days, but the period remains to be established with greater precision for this species. The following year a new site was found, but the nest was so large that it could not have been a single year's construction; possibly it was the missing 1963 nest. In the last week in August it contained an eaglet about four weeks old. We noticed that it was breathing stertorously and found that a large maggot-like larva of the Tropical Nest Fly *Passeromyia heterochaeta* blocked one nostril. I removed the parasite and sent it off for identification. Subsequently maggots of this fly have been found in the nostrils of several eagle species and other birds of prey.

Three years passed before they used this nest again. A hide was constructed in a small tree 15 metres away and I looked forward to obtaining some striking studies

. . . and reveals her massive wing spread.

with a 500 mm lens once the eaglet had hatched. However, when I made a routine check during the incubation period, I found that the egg had unaccountably disappeared. My bitter disappointment may well be imagined, but the copious lining of fresh green leaves in the nest led me to play a hunch. I stayed away from the nest for a month before returning in mid-July to find that they had laid another egg. Although egg-collectors claim that eagles readily re-lay if their eggs are taken, this was one of the very few instances in my own experience where an eagle has laid again.

I left Rhodesia on leave soon after this welcome discovery, but when I returned at the beginning of October it was to find that the egg had failed to hatch. It had been incubated for seventy-four days since it was found, well beyond the time it should have hatched. There was no harm in attempting some photography at that stage, so I set up the camera in the hide and settled down to await developments.

Magnificent Martial: the female in a bold pose.

After fifty minutes the male came to the nest, just as I was beginning to think that they had given up the fruitless task of incubation on the very day I hoped to obtain at least a few pictures. Once settled, he sat virtually immobile for almost an hour, except for some ludicrous attempts to catch an annoying fly with his bill. Then the female was heard nearby calling softly, and the male left as she came to replace him. She ignored the lens, just as the male had done, and paused at the back of the nest. Through the viewfinder she was impressive beyond words as she stood sharply etched against an out of focus backdrop of the hill across the valley.

For a magnificent moment she posed before settling, and almost with the reverence of a worshipper I released the shutter. In that instant I obtained the eagle portrait of my lifetime.

8 *An African Hawk-Eagle's World*

Visualize an expanse of flaxen grass dotted with rusty-leaved trees and bushes. As we proceed over a slight rise a huge green acacia looms into view, and in one of its upper forks is a large nest of sticks. Hanging from the outer branches are a few coarsely woven nests of Red-headed Weavers, one of the many examples of the "association" between weavers and nesting eagles. It is the beginning of September 1961, and with Tim Longden, who showed me the site on Longridge Ranch, I look up at the nest above me, my second eagle's nest in Rhodesia. I throw up a dead branch which clatters against the main trunk, and the female African Hawk-Eagle bursts off the nest to reveal a white breast and abdomen which are heavily streaked with black; it is from this that the specific name *spilogaster* is derived, literally "spotted stomach". Then, banking, she displayed the characteristic "windows" near the wing tips which are the easiest guide to identification. The smaller Ayres' Hawk-Eagle lacks these windows, and the underwing is heavily barred, so it should not be mistaken for an African Hawk-Eagle if a good view is obtained. It is an unaccountably rare eagle which I have only seen twice, although I did keep an injured female for a while before releasing it.

The bird overhead looked every bit an eagle to me, so it was difficult to understand the prefix "Hawk". Apparently this is yet another hangover from the time when early taxonomists didn't really know what they were about, so they invented crossbreeds to mask their indecision. It is not generally known these days that we used to have Crowned Hawk-Eagle and Martial Hawk-Eagle too, but the "Hawk" has sensibly been allowed to lapse, a course which would prove ridiculous if applied to the African Hawk-Eagle.

The first branch was three metres above us, so I threw a rope over it and hauled myself up. The rest was not difficult, and soon I was ten metres above ground looking into the nest which contained a single egg handsomely blotched with rust-red. For their size these eagles construct a substantial nest, and the sticks used are large too; in this case it was a metre across the top with the usual lining of green leaves. From the nest I looked about for a place for a hide, but there was no suitable position from which to overlook it. In any case, some weeks later, incubation had been abandoned, so I took the egg and found that it was infertile. In subsequent years I established that the African Hawk-Eagles at Essexvale laid in the first half of June, so the egg had probably been incubated for nearly three months, or for twice the length of the incubation period. When I blew the egg the stench certainly supported this supposition!

The following year I located another nest in a remote spot on the Mulungwane hills. It was placed in the fork of a small tree a mere four metres above ground, and it is the lowest nest of this species on record. We constructed a small pylon

The Longridge African Hawk-Eagle's eyrie was situated in a fine specimen of Acacia albida: *Red-headed Weaver nests may be seen hanging on the right.*

The rickety pylon hide at the site on the Mulungwane hills: this is an unusually low nest for an African Hawk-Eagle.

88

hide on the slope which gave a good vantage point for photography and used local timber for the job. When complete, it had the distinction of being the most rickety hide I have ever built, with a marked propensity to topple forward onto its face. But it worked, and I spent many hours in it with nothing before me except the incubating eagle and an unbroken vista of lonely land.

The eggs were incubated almost continuously during my watches, the main bulk of this task being undertaken by the female who showed her complete lack of suspicion of the hide by falling asleep on a number of occasions. Occasionally she stood to turn the eggs or rearrange nest lining, otherwise she sat placidly for long periods. Thus it was that I was startled out of a daydream one afternoon when she called to the male and then left. A little while later he came to the nest, and I noticed immediately that he was less heavily streaked than his mate. His crop was bulging from a recent feed, and he had presumably given the female the balance of the prey. This was borne out when she returned half an hour later with a full crop to resume incubation. The male relieved the female on another occasion too, so it seems that he participates in incubation while the female is away feeding on prey which he has brought for her. His role as provider of food during incubation is a vital one, for his mate is virtually tied to the nest.

When incubation extended into August I began to suspect that the eggs were infertile, and in the second week the nest was deserted. Again I found that the eggs were watery and rotten within, and I began to wonder when I would be privileged to see my first eaglet. It turned out that the "Mulungwane" pair, as I called them, were to have a most unfortunate breeding history for in ten years they were not known to have reared a single eaglet. Unlike the "Longridge" pair, they moved to new nest sites a number of times, having four in all, although only three of these were used to my knowledge. They laid a single egg in several years, but none of these hatched; at other times they apparently did not attempt to breed at all. Once one egg of a two egg clutch was infertile, but the other hatched. Success was short-lived, however, for the whole nest was pushed out of the tree, presumably by an African with a grudge against them. Perhaps they were taking his chickens, but I never had enough opportunity to find out from remains on the nest whether this was in fact the case. On the few occasions that I found prey it was always some species of francolin, and once there were five Swainson's Francolins, three adults and two young birds, on the nest at one time. As I found out later at the Longridge nest, African Hawk-Eagles prey mostly on birds, particularly francolins.

Six years later the Mulungwane pair used the same site and hatched two young, but again the whole nest was pushed out of the tree, possibly by the same vindictive person. I had taken the smaller eaglet for hand rearing before this catastrophe, but misfortune seemed to follow it. I placed it in a box beside that of the Tawny eaglet I was rearing, and one morning it accidently fell into the Tawny's box. By the time I discovered this, it had been pecked to death. It is worth noting here that its down colour was grey (a Tawny eaglet's is white) but this did not prevent the Tawny's attack. Perhaps there is something for the behaviourists in this, for it seems that movement and not down colour acts as the "releaser" for sibling aggression.

The birth of an African Hawk-Eagle.

The Mulungwane pair's record was indeed a gloomy one, but on the credit side, in one of the two years that they hatched eggs, I was able to establish that the incubation period was 42–43 days. It is of interest to mention here that the female attacked me occasionally, one of the few instances in my own experience of an attack by any species of eagle. No actual strike took place, but once it was a near thing, and only a waved arm and shout put the female off in the nick of time.

The Longridge pair's breeding performance was, happily, an excellent one, for in eleven years they reared nine young. In one year they did not breed and, as mentioned earlier, their egg did not hatch in 1961. They continued to use the 1961 site until 1964, but there was no sign of them the following year. The nest did not appear to have been repaired, but I asked my African assistant, Douglas, to pop up and check the condition of the nest anyway. Meanwhile I fossicked around below to see if there were any prey remains. Suddenly there was an anguished yell from above, and Douglas was clearly in retreat down the tree. It took some while before the "Aahs" were replaced by intelligible speech, but then I was able to appreciate that the poor fellow had had a frightening experience. Looking up through binoculars I saw a medium sized python coiled up in the sticks at the base of the nest; unfortunate Douglas had only seen it when he was in mid stride towards the nest branch and, knowing an African's terror of snakes, I'm amazed that he didn't jump headlong from the tree then and there.

It is difficult to know whether the presence of the python had inhibited breeding that year, but somehow I doubt it; a more likely explanation is that the python was there because the birds were absent. However, they returned in 1966, and built a new nest on a lateral branch on the opposite side of the tree. The reason for the move is uncertain, but they may have been having difficulty in securing the old nest in position; it is perhaps significant that it soon fell down. From my point of view the move could not have been better, but I refrained from building a hide in an excellent position until the following year. Instead I made weekly visits to the nest to record the growth and development of the eaglet, something which I had been unable to do on a regular basis in previous years. When first hatched the eaglet is covered in dark grey down, but by two weeks most of this has been replaced by whitish down, except for some grey which remains on the back and the top of the head. First feathers appear at three weeks, after which there is a feather explosion until it is virtually covered by feathers at six weeks.

The following year, before the birds had even begun to repair the nest, I built a hide against the main trunk five metres away. Where the lens was to protrude, I nailed a shiny tin in position to ensure that they would not be camera shy when it came to the real thing. As it turned out, they were almost embarrassingly tame, and when the necessity arose I could put my hand outside the hide to make adjustments to equipment without arousing more than a brief glance. Over the next four years I spent many hours studying their ways, my hide being merely part of the tree as far as they were concerned. The account of their breeding cycle which follows is a composite picture drawn from a mass of notes, but I doubt whether I shall ever tire of watching them.

The female African Hawk-Eagle alights at the Mulungwane nest and shows the distinctive flight pattern of the species.

It is early April when I throw a rope over that first branch, which is worn smooth from hundreds of ascents, and each handhold on the way up to the hide is as familiar to me as the books on my library shelves. Looking across I can see that no repair has yet taken place, for the nest is as flat as it was when the eaglet left the previous year. Later, at the beginning of May, the first sticks have been added to the perimeter, and now it is time to begin some watches from the hide to study their building activity.

The camera is ready to record any important details as I settle down with a good book to await developments. All is quiet for nearly two hours until noisy broken-voiced "kwee-u, kwee-u" calls herald the female's arrival in the tree, followed shortly afterwards by the male. Now she intersperses her screaming cries with softer "kwi, kwi"

My view of the Longridge nest from the hide . . .

. . . and the African Hawk-Eagles' view of the hide.

93

The male African Hawk-Eagle about to place a stick on the rim of the nest.

notes which have an almost "conversational" quality. Then she falls silent and perches on a favourite branch behind the nest, while her mate bounds from branch to branch looking for a dead stick to break off for the nest. Having found one, he accidentally drops it. Then he comes to the nest without a stick and tramps about pulling at various sticks before placing one in a new position. Meanwhile the female preens and takes no apparent interest. After a while, as if on a signal, they fly from the tree together. Shortly afterwards the female is back with a large spray of leaves which she merely drops in the nest cup before jumping to her perch at the back of the nest. Then the male returns to the nest, again without material, arranges a few sticks, and presses his breast into the leaves in the centre to shape the bowl. After this he flies from the nest tree, followed by the female a while later, and although I wait another three and a half hours before departing, neither of them is seen again. During a spell of nearly six hours in the hide, they have been on or near the nest for only forty-five minutes.

When I visited the nest five weeks later it was well built up, and within two weeks eggs were to be laid in it. Observations began at 8.30 a.m., but it was an hour before the eagles arrived in the tree. The male jumped down to the nest where he pushed his breast into the leaves in the centre and kicked backwards with his outstretched feet with a pedalling motion. This was accompanied by musical "kwip, kwip" notes which the female answered with a soft clucking. Then the male flew up directly

The female's contribution to the preparation of the nest is a large spray of greenery.

The female African Hawk-Eagle, feathers fluffed out, settles to incubate her two eggs.

She may sit in the same position for hours on end.

96

But when someone approaches she peers intently over her shoulders . . .

. . . and moments later flattens herself into the nest cup.

97

Portrait of a captive female Ayres' Hawk-Eagle.

The female African Hawk-Eagle with her three week old eaglet.

to land beside her and they mated; she held her body in a crouching position with her back horizontal and tail held to one side, and he mounted her with his abdomen lowered and feathers fluffed out, a position very similar to that assumed when eagles bathe. The union lasted about half a minute, and when it was over the male flew from the nest tree.

The female remained on her perch, and twenty minutes later the male returned. He broke off a dead stick from the tree, brought it to the nest in his bill, and placed it in position. Then he picked up and dropped various pieces of nest material, obviously very excited, but the female took no notice of his behaviour. A while later he flew up to her, and once more they mated. He left the tree to return nearly an hour later with a small mouse in his talons. The female rent the air with her cries of solicitation, but he went directly to the nest and waited until she came to take it from him there. She flew off with it to eat it elsewhere, and he remained in the tree preening until she returned. After this there was no further activity, so I left the hide at one o'clock.

The length of time taken to complete nest repair varied in different years; it was usually about a month, but once it took two months. So far I have not been in the hide to witness an egg being laid, and it is an event that I hope to be lucky enough to see one day. On the only occasion where I was able to establish laying with reasonable accuracy, the egg was laid some time after 3 p.m. in the afternoon and before 10.30 a.m. the following morning. The eggs that I have seen were usually well marked, but in a clutch of two they were never alike, and one egg would always be more heavily blotched. The Mulungwane pair laid a single egg on three occasions, but at the Longridge nest, except for the one egg in the first year, the clutch was always two. This is the usual clutch for this species, but very occasionally three eggs have been recorded, and I have once seen a nest with three eggs in the Matopos.

The incubation period of eagles, as I have already indicated, is an uneventful time for the observer. Those with a penchant for particularly detailed notes may be kept reasonably occupied by noting each time the bird moves to face a different direction, or preens, or yawns, but such activities are of little significance to my way of thinking, and I confine my notes to recording periods of absence from the nest, or visits by the male. It is a good time to catch up on one's reading, for the incubating bird will alert one for any action by calling to its mate.

In contrast to the inactivity of the eagle, there is a constant traffic of birds through the tree. Being the largest tree in the area, it seems to be used as a feeding or stopping off point by a wide variety of species. For my own amusement I have kept a record of birds seen, and each time I spend a day in the hide the list seems to grow. The hide is merely part of the tree as far as the passing birds are concerned, and I have had some delightfully intimate views of them. Once a Bearded Woodpecker tapped away at a dead branch so close that I could have reached out and touched it. Amongst regular visitors to the tree are hoopoes, hornbills, barbets, shrikes, glossy starlings and sunbirds. The eagle seems to arouse no animosity and many birds forage nearby, sometimes even in the sticks of the nest itself. A group of cackling Red-billed Hoopoes searched for food all round the nest on one occasion, and they certainly have one of the most suitable African names I know – "Hlekabafazi" – which is Ndebele

The male African Hawk-Eagle perched behind the nest after delivering prey.

for "laughter of women". One of my favourites, on account of its melodious call, is the Black-headed Oriole, whose notes are like a cascade of liquid gold. Occasionally a sharp snort carries up from below, and a herd of impala is seen threading its way through the bushes not far from the tree. Sometimes I just think, a relaxation which modern man has very little time to indulge. At such times one's imagination becomes sharpened, and I begin to wonder how old the tree is, and what changes and what sights it has experienced. For all I know it may have heard the murmur of Matabele warriors, and the scuff of their bare feet, as they passed to attack Selous' house not far away.

Eventually the day comes when the eaglet is heard cheeping inside the shell, although

101

no fracture of the surface is yet visible. This is at 10 a.m., and three hours later a slight crack is noticed near the top of the egg. Once the female stood up and looked down for some while at the eggs between her feet, apparently well aware that hatching was not far off. At three o'clock the next afternoon there was a small hole in the shell through which the eaglet's bill was clearly visible, but it needed to struggle some while yet before it would be free of the egg. Twenty-four hours later the eaglet is hatched and dry, and there are no remains of shell on the nest. It is able to hold up its relatively huge head for short periods, and its eyes are weakly open and watery. Despite its apparent helplessness, it has already been fed a full crop from a Swainson's Francolin which lies on the nest. In these early days the female is constantly in attendance brooding or feeding the eaglet, and the male brings in prey.

Three days later the second egg hatches, and the new eaglet is half the weight of the older one. Soon it is persistently pecked, and the ensuing struggle, summed up effectively in the words of Leslie Brown, is "as unequal a contest as one between a strong and active heavyweight boxer and a lightweight just out of a hospital bed". Usually, if I am in time, sentiment prevails, and I rescue the small eaglet from almost certain death by removing it for rearing. I have no personal experience of two young being raised successfully together, but observations in Kenya have established that two may be reared at times. The surviving eaglet watched that year was precocious in its development, and at five days old had sufficient co-ordination to preen itself. When two weeks old it was able to shuffle about on bent legs, and while being fed by the female it made clumsy attempts to tear off food on its own, even clutching at the prey with its claws.

By the time it is two weeks old, the eaglet no longer requires constant attention, but the female is usually present on or near the nest. Sometimes she leaves the tree, and one has to be alert to note her return. Once on a quiet windless day she landed above the hide without a sound; only when she ruffled her feathers did I realise that she was there. Presumably, like the Crowned Eagle, silent flight is an asset in surprise attack. One of the factors which releases her from the nest is that it is in shade most of the time. If the sun is on the nest at any stage, and the eaglet is distressed, she will either stand so that it may lie in her shadow, or crouch over it.

The tranquil scene is broken in the middle of the morning by the staccato "Gweh" calls of Grey Loeries. Their notes have a particular quality that indicates their alarm, so I know that the male's arrival with prey is imminent. The female strikes up with her raucous cries of solicitation, and the male lands with a Coqui Francolin. He emits a few soft notes, but they are drowned by his mate: at such a time one cannot help making a comparison with the world of humans. There is no mantling by the female, and after a few minutes together he flies up to perch beside the hide. His plumage is immaculate when viewed at close range, and he is quite the most dapper male eagle I know. Once, as he was perched to one side of the hide, I was able to cut a hole in the sacking, stick the lens out, and secure his portrait.

While he settles down to preen, the female turns her attention to feeding the eaglet

The female African Hawk-Eagle on a favourite perch behind the nest.

The male brings a mongoose to the nest for the 11 day old eaglet. He has already fed on the foreparts himself and his crop is bulging.

103

The female African Hawk-Eagle stands beside her three week old eaglet . . .

which has been cheeping insistently since prey was delivered. The francolin is already thoroughly plucked, and the male's full crop explains why only the rear half has been brought. Holding it down with the inside toe of each foot, she tears off pieces which are swallowed in rapid succession by the hungry eaglet. After eighteen minutes it has been fed to satiety, and it turns its back on further morsels which are offered. Feeding ceased at 10.30 a.m., and it was not fed again until two o'clock. On completion of the meal, the female cleaned the nest meticulously of any portions that had gone astray; during the clean-up she noted that some flesh was stuck to the side of the eaglet's face, so she gently pecked this off. Then she crouched over the eaglet which fell asleep beneath her, but after a while she was annoyed by a fly on the nest and made a sudden lunge at it her her bill. The eaglet shot into wakefulness in the most comical way, looked about blearily for the cause of the disturbance, and fixed its gaze on the hide where I was unable to suppress a chuckle.

The following week the three week old eaglet had a full crop when I started observations at 8.45 a.m., and the plucked carcasses of two Coqui Francolins lay beside it. No adults were seen when I arrived, and it spent much of its time preening or shuffling about; when the sun fell on it, the eaglet merely moved into a patch of shade on the edge of the nest. The female returned an hour later and perched behind the hide, where she had a long preen before resting her foot. This is a position quite often adopted by eagles; they take their weight on one leg and bend the other

. . . then settles to brood it.

The eaglet stands and turns to defecate over the nest edge.

and rest it on the branch. It was an impressive pose, so I carefully cut a hole in the back of the hide, stuck the lens out, and obtained a number of pictures without disturbing her. It was evident that the eaglet was now being left unattended for much longer periods, although the female was still present in the tree for most of the time. After an hour she flew down to the nest, crouched with the eaglet in front of her, and proceeded to preen it, nibbling the down of its neck, back and head. While I had watched eaglets of other species being preened for brief periods before, this was the first time that I had seen it carried out with such thoroughness and for so long. Her attentions only broke off when the eaglet stood up, aimed his posterior for the edge and defecated. Despite the two francolins available, it was not fed in the two hours that the female was on the nest. When I was fetched from the hide she lay flat, but the eaglet had not yet developed this reaction, so it merely sat up in full view beside her looking about.

Three days later, when it was twenty-four days old, it crouched flat when it saw me climbing to the hide. Soon both male and female returned to the tree, the female perching on a branch behind the nest and the male on one near the hide. He remained there for an hour and a half before flying away, but she didn't move until noon, nearly four hours after observations started. During all this time the eaglet slept, preened, or stood weakly to attempt a few clumsy wing flaps. She eventually flew from the tree, and when she returned five minutes later the male accompanied her. Both resumed their favourite perches, but after twenty minutes the male flew off,

Once it has settled again the female gives it a thorough preening.

This portrait of the female African Hawk-Eagle leaving the nest shows her lethal talons well.

The female African Hawk-Eagle with the thirty-one day old eaglet which is feathering rapidly.

not to be seen again that afternoon. It was nearly three hours before the female came to the nest, and she fed the eaglet on a dove which had been lying there since my arrival. The prey was demolished in twelve minutes, then she crouched beside the eaglet which nibbled her toes and legs. Forty minutes later she left, not returning by the time I left at 4.30 p.m. I had been eight hours in the hide, and although she had been present most of the time, only an hour of this was spent on the nest.

A week later, when the eaglet was thirty-one days old, I watched for four hours, commencing at 8.45 a.m. The eaglet was obviously hungry, and called with a monotonous "wee-yik, wee-yik" for much of the time, but the female only arrived at eleven o'clock carrying the head of a hare. Most of the flesh had been eaten off this, but she gave the eaglet what she could find, as well as pieces of bone. The strength of her twisting pecks was evident, and I could hear the scrunching of bone as she broke up the skull. The eaglet was given a few pieces of bone which it swallowed, but some unmanageable pieces were rejected and gulped down by the female instead. Once the eaglet stood, grasped the skull, and tried to tear off pieces itself. Its attempt was unsuccessful, but had the prey been a bird I'm sure it would have been able to feed itself. Apart from this unrewarding meal, the eaglet was left unattended. Its feathers were beginning to appear rapidly through the down at this stage, and it was to be left increasingly to its own devices. It walked round the nest quite a bit, although still a little unsure of its balance.

Ten days later the eaglet was covered by feathers, a rapid transformation in so short a period. During the morning the female arrived with a francolin which she fed to the eaglet. It grasped the prey in its foot and tried to feed itself, but she merely continued to tear off pieces for it herself. When she left to perch in the tree, the eaglet walked around the nest, now sure of its balance, and did some wing exercises.

Parental visits were now mainly concerned with the delivery of prey, but the adults still continued to perch in the tree from time to time. Once during a four hour watch when the eaglet was fifty days old, both birds were in the tree for much of the time. Although the eaglet appeared to be hungry, and called to them for food, they took virtually no notice of it. With its full covering of feathers it was an attractive eaglet, dark brown above and chestnut below, with some streaking on the breast, but it would take three to four years before it assumed full adult coloration. Wing exercises were now a frequent occurrence, and it made mock kills at times by pouncing on a stick and clutching it with its talons. Then there were various activities which ornithologists have termed "comfort movements and maintenance activities". The main ones of the eaglet were stretching, foot-resting and preening; I derived considerable enjoyment from making a full photographic record of these and obtained some interesting poses. Preening is particularly important, for the feathers are still breaking from the quills and the eaglet removes the pieces of dry sheath from them as they emerge. There are also what may be termed "boredom activities". This mainly takes the form of nibbling at the nest sticks or fiddling with dry lining; sometimes the eaglet may pick up a dry bone and juggle it about in its bill before dropping it, often to be picked up again. These pastimes appear purposeless, but they are all part of the eaglet's increasing co-ordination and "exploration" of its environment.

110

The forty day old eaglet, now covered by feathers, grasps the prey when the female does not start feeding it.

Soon the day of its first flight approaches. Initially it practises a few short flights across the nest, and much of its time is spent perching on the highest point it can find on the rim of the nest. Next it becomes a "brancher", a term used in falconry for a bird of prey, usually a sparrowhawk, which is perched near its nest but hasn't yet made its first sustained flight. I take fledging to mean the eaglet's first sustained flight from the tree, and I was able to obtain this fairly accurately in one case. At four o'clock on the afternoon of its sixty-eighth day it was perched on a branch above the nest, and when I returned at 9 a.m. the following morning it had gone. On another occasion I climbed to the nest when the eaglet was sixty-one days old, but found it gone. As I was inspecting prey remains, it suddenly took off from foliage

Some activities of the seven week old African Hawk-Eagle: here it exercises its wings.

The left wing and foot are stretched simultaneously.

112

The tip of its tail receives attention during preening.

Resting its foot on which a ring may be seen.

113

The pair of African Hawk-Eagles on their nest, the more heavily streaked female is behind.

on the edge of the tree, where it had been hidden from my view, and flew strongly for 200 metres before I lost sight of it. I had probably caused it to fly prematurely, but its competence on the wing suggested that it would have fledged naturally within a day or two. In another year fledging was not in excess of sixty-five days, so the period is a short one, usually less than that of Wahlberg's Eagle, a species of much the same size.

I was able to obtain some observations on the post-fledging period one year, and initially the young eagle returned to receive prey on the nest. Each time I would clear away all the prey remains, so that by the following visit it would be possible to see whether the eyrie was still being used as a feeding point. It was on the nest

A portrait of the male African Hawk-Eagle.

The African Hawk-Eagles in flight over the nest: the smaller male is below.

The female African Hawk-Eagle rests her foot on a perch behind the hide.

with prey eleven days after fledging, and a week later both male and female were in the tree and the juvenile was feeding on the nest; interestingly it adopted the intruder position, and only flew off when I was half way up the tree. Three weeks later there was no sign of prey, and the condition of the nest was rapidly deteriorating. Thus it appears that the young bird returns for the first few weeks, but soon becomes independent of the nest. I know nothing of what becomes of it after this, and one can only surmise that it wanders further afield with its parents before becoming fully independent.

The eaglet usually leaves the nest at the end of September, just as Wahlberg's Eagles are laying, and a month or so later the first rains break. The tree, the focal point of the African Hawk-Eagle's world, watches the birth and growth of green grass, and its inevitable autumnal fading to yellow. This is how it has been during the tree's existence down the span of years, and it stands through the blend and blur of the seasons like a symbol of immutable strength.

Then the day comes when the eagles begin to repair the nest, and once again the rasp of a rough rope thrown over that first branch is heard. There is, of course, always more to be learnt about the life of the eagles, but not all that much. No, it is no longer the quest for knowledge which draws me to that tree; something which I can not adequately explain has penetrated to my very soul. All I know is that as long as I have the strength I shall continue to haul myself up to that tree-top world.

9 *Snake Eagles*

Of all the eagles I have studied, the Snake Eagles fascinate me the most. They are by no means spectacular birds, but I have been able to study two African species more intimately than anyone else, so it is only natural that I should have a particularly soft spot for them. There are four species in southern Africa: the Southern Banded Snake Eagle, Banded Snake Eagle, Black-breasted Snake Eagle and Brown Snake Eagle; the last two I know well, but the ''Banded'' ones are very poorly known anywhere in Africa and nothing worthwile has been found out about their breeding biology.

The Southern Banded Snake Eagle is chiefly recognizable by the barring on its lower breast and abdomen, and by the three black bands on the tail; the illustration in ''Roberts'' is a good one. Its distribution is mainly on the eastern littoral from Natal northwards to Kenya, but it also occurs in some localities in eastern Rhodesia. For a great many years I had hoped to encounter this species, but it eluded me until it was one of the few southern African birds of prey, and the last eagle, I had yet to see. Then, recently, came the memorable day in Ndumu Game Reserve in Zululand when I spotted one, and recognized it immediately. Kipling would have approved of the setting, a clearing in thick woodland ''all set about with fever-trees'', on the edge of which it perched.

The Banded Snake Eagle occurs in southern Africa along the Zambezi-Chobe river systems, and it is a dull version of the Southern Banded with indistinct barring on the abdomen. The best single identification feature is the broad white band across the tail when it flies. I have had experience of this species in the Chobe Game Reserve in Botswana, where there is always a fair chance of seeing one. On my first visit to Chobe, together with Ken Newman, I was fortunate to obtain some photographs of one which obligingly perched near the road early one morning. It is usually unobtrusive, spending most of its time perched in riverine woodland, often near or even over water. In view of this it is significant that, besides snakes, fish and frogs have been recorded in its diet. One that I watched at Chobe for one and a half hours was perched in a tree over the river where it remained virtually immobile.

Both the Brown and Black-breasted Snake Eagles are more widely distributed; the former tends to be found in woodland and the latter in open savannah, but it is difficult to generalise, and they overlap a great deal. To my mind they are better separated on an ecological basis by their distinctly different hunting methods which will be discussed more fully later.

Until quite recently these eagles were called ''Harrier-Eagles'' because of a supposed similarity to the harriers, but any harrier-like features which exist are purely superficial, and most recent writers have adopted the name Snake Eagle. As they are specialized

119

A Banded Snake Eagle photographed in the Chobe Game Reserve.

A Brown Snake Eagle in a typical upright still-hunting posture.

The hide at the Brown Snake Eagle's nest in 1962: the nest is arrowed.

From below this Black-breasted Snake Eagle's nest on top of a euphorbia would be almost impossible to detect.

This nest of a Black-breasted Snake Eagle shows the flimsy nature of Snake Eagle nests.

123

to deal with snakes, the recent trend is a sound one, but the generic name *Circaetus*, a mixture of Latin and Greek, remains as a reminder of the old name.

What, then, are the features which characterize Snake Eagles and make them different from other eagles? In the first instance they have very small feet, and these, as well as the unfeathered legs, are heavily scaled for protection against the bites of snakes. The claws are relatively short and not particularly sharp, but the inside of the foot is rough for holding smooth quarry. The thick pad of down beneath the body feathers, while not confined to Snake Eagles alone, gives further protection from bites. All four species have rounded heads with loose feathers at the back which, combined with their large yellow eyes, gives them a rather owl-like appearance. They have keen eyesight, and a hovering Black-breasted Snake Eagle has been known to attack prey from a height of 500 metres. Their hunting methods fall into two distinct categories: the two Banded species and the Brown are still-hunters, perching for long periods surveying the ground beneath them, but the Brown has occasionally been known to quarter the ground and even to hover briefly. The Black-breasted Snake Eagle does virtually all its hunting on the wing; often it hovers for sustained periods on winnowing wings at the point of a stall like a giant kestrel or Black-shouldered Kite, and its general similarity to the Martial Eagle has resulted in the belief that Martials hover quite frequently too, but this is a rare occurrence.

So far as it is known, all species merely swoop down on a snake and grab it, apparently with no particular attempt to hold it behind the head. Although the feet are small, their clutch is immensely powerful, and the snake is crippled by the vice-like grip. The eagle also gives twisting pecks to the spine which further incapacitate the victim. An incident in Zambia illustrates the ability of these eagles to cope with snakes: a Brown Snake Eagle, which is not a particularly large eagle, although largest of the Snake Eagles, was encountered in the final stages of killing a Black Mamba nearly three metres long. The Game Warden who recorded this epic battle, the marks of which were spread over some twenty metres of dirt road, wrote that the mamba was "still writhing vigorously and striking blindly, while the eagle, with wings half open, was pecking and tearing at it".

Snake Eagles are not immune to the venom of snakes, and the two species which I have studied kill Boomslangs, adders and cobras, including the Black-necked Cobra which is a spitting variety. One can only surmise that, when dealing with "spitters", their eyes are protected by the nictitating membrane which can be drawn across the eye instantaneously. Thus they are exposed to, and ingest, the three main types of snake venoms. There is no evidence to suggest that they distinguish and avoid venomous varieties, most of the snakes brought to nests at Essexvale were venomous, so it is clear that they are efficient killers. I have often wondered how they avoid the effects of the venom they swallow, because I have seen all three snake types I have mentioned swallowed with their heads on. A friend who is an expert on snakes told me that a human can drink snake venom without any ill effects, as long as he has no sores in his mouth, or ulcers or other internal wounds. When I asked him to give me a demonstration he declined, pleading possible ulcers, but he affirmed that a healthy person, or eagle, could do so.

124

A week old Brown Snake Eagle chick.

By four weeks old feathers are developing rapidly and the dark eye has changed to yellow.

At six weeks it has an effective covering of feathers and no longer needs to be shaded.

125

The female Brown Snake Eagle returns to the nest with a spray of green leaves to relieve the male who has been shading the eaglet during her absence.

The male Brown Snake Eagle comes to the nest with the tail of a leguaan which the female pulls out of his mouth.

The 67 day old eaglet pulls a large Puff Adder from the throat of the male.

The female Brown Snake Eagle feeds the twelve day old eaglet on small pieces torn off a snake.

Most eagles regurgitate pellets in which undigested bones are cast up, wrapped in the fur or feathers of their prey. However, apart from a few very small pellets of scales occasionally found on nests, it seems that snakes are almost entirely digested by Snake Eagles. This is confirmed by the nature of their excreta too, at least as far as eaglets are concerned, which is of a solid nature and has the consistency of a calcium tablet when dry. Also, they do not "jet" over the edge of the nest as do other eaglets and droppings usually land on the rim or just over it.

Another interesting aspect of their adaption to a diet made up mainly of snakes is their ability to swallow large ones, and I know from my own observations that the Brown Snake Eagle can swallow a snake at least 150 centimetres long, or a

Puff Adder as thick as a man's arm. Remarkably, after such Gargantuan meals, there is no sign of a bulge in the crop, the reason being that the snake passes straight down to the stomach. I only discovered this when I kept an immature Black-breasted Snake Eagle for nearly two years. If I fed it rats, birds or butcher's meat, it developed a bulging crop, just as a normal eagle would. When it was fed on snakes, however, the crop would not expand, instead a taut bulge could be felt between its legs.

The Black-breasted Snake Eagle is capable of swallowing snakes in flight, and I have witnessed the process on a number of occasions. The feet are brought forward, the bird's head is bent down and the snake's head is grasped with the bill. Then it is gulped down, while the feet feed it along like a sort of airborne conveyer belt. Once I saw one in flight swallow a snake about a metre long, and then pull it out of its mouth again with its feet; the eagle seemed to be having problems of adjustment because the swallowing and extraction process was repeated no fewer than six times! It is in context to mention here that I know of no evidence to suggest that snakes are dropped to kill them, as is stated in one reputable book on snakes.

A final point about the diet of Snake Eagles is their impressive capacity for snakes. One observer records a Brown Snake Eagle "gorged to the chin with two large snakes, each at least four feet long, and swallowed whole". Another states that he found four snakes inside one he shot which were "all different kinds of ground and tree snakes, measuring eighteen to thirty inches in length".

The habits and adaptions of Snake Eagles with regard to their prey are fascinating, but their breeding biology is also extremely interesting and exhibits certain differences from other eagles. I have studied two nests of the Brown Snake Eagle and one of the Black-breasted, and I propose to outline the breeding cycle of the Brown, the species I know most intimately. The nesting habits of the Black-breasted Snake Eagles are basically similar, and I shall later draw attention to such differences that exist.

If an observer wants to study the full breeding cycle of the Brown Snake Eagle, then he is committed to a period of just over two hundred days. This extends from the time of first nest repair until the eaglet no longer returns to the nest. In the two years that I watched Brown Snake Eagle nests I clocked up a total of 156 hours' observation. While this does not sound much, it was all spent perched in small pylon hides and it is impossible to compute this in terms of cramped limbs and a stiff neck. Yet I would do it all again, and much more, for just half the interest of those long hours.

The Brown Snake Eagles I studied in a sporadic fashion from 1961 to 1972 nested over an area of about 250 hectares on the Mulungwane hills not far from the first African Hawk-Eagle I photographed. I could not find the nest, if they were breeding, in 1963 and during the period 1966 to 1970; in the remaining six years they laid eggs and reared four young. It should be mentioned here that despite statements of a clutch of two mentioned in some bird books, there is no reliable evidence that this species, or the Black-breasted, ever lays more than one egg. My detailed studies were made in 1962 and 1971, and my remarks on activity at the nest are a synthesis of the two. If is very difficult to know whether the same birds were involved in both years; on his behaviour the 1971 male would not appear to have been the same as the 1962 one. The sexes can not usually be distinguished, but fortunately the 1971 female had a broader white band at the tip of her tail than the male, as well as a new outer tail feather growing down, and so she was easily recognized.

The schoolboy who originally found it brought me an excited account of a "Crowned" Eagle's nest, and as soon as the first weekend came we set off to walk the five kilometres to the site. When he pointed out the nest my doubts about his identification were confirmed, for on top of a low thorn tree was the frame of a small stick nest a mere 60 centimetres across. The nest was still being constructed but when a brown eagle in the distance revealed dark underwing coverts contrasting with white flight feathers, as well as three clear white bars on the tail, I knew whose nest it was. My informant was rather dejected at the metamorphosis of his "Crowned", but I assured him that his discovery was much more valuable because the Crowned Eagle had been thoroughly studied, while the Brown Snake Eagle had not.

The nest was on a hillside near the top of the Mulungwanes, and from where we stood I could see the faint impression of a track that had been used in the early gold mining days. I calculated that it would link up with a farm road I knew, and thus give me access by Land Rover to the nest area. This turned out to be the case, and I was spared having to carry materials for a hide over five kilometres of rough country.

The construction of the nest took about a month, and the large white egg was laid at the end of December. I thought that it was somewhat unusual for the eagle to lay at the height of the rainy season, but in subsequent years I found that they laid consistently at this time, usually during January. Furthermore, from the few reliable records I could find, it seems that this breeding season is constant in southern Africa. In contrast, the Black-breasted Snake Eagle lays, on present information, in most months. Why one species should breed consistently at one time of the year, and the other at a variety of times, remains a problem to be solved. It is relevant to mention here that the Bateleur, at least in Rhodesia, matches the breeding season of the Brown Snake Eagle very closely, and thus both species would have their young in the nest during the cool, dry winter months.

One of the problems of studying Snake Eagles at Essexvale was the difficulty of finding their nests, for they frequently moved to new nest sites. The nests are small, and usually placed on top of a thorn tree in leaf. Once, in the Matopos, I saw a Black-breasted Snake Eagle's nest on top of a euphorbia; in such a situation it is impossible to detect unless one sees the bird flying to it. Rarely, in the case of the Brown Snake Eagle, the nest may be situated in a fork of a tree beneath the canopy, and occasionally the old nest of another bird of prey is used. During incubation and the early part of the fledging period, the intruder position is adopted on the approach of an observer, and often it is maintained to extraordinary lengths, even if one is in full view of the nest only a short distance away. This behaviour means that one could walk past a nest situated on top of a thickly foliaged thorn tree without seeing it.

The female covers the egg for long periods without a break and the male brings food for her, although he has not been seen to do any incubation. Perhaps, if protracted watches were made, he may yet be found to relieve the female for short periods

A female Black-breasted Snake Eagle brings a Yellow-bellied Grass Snake to her nest on top of a euphorbia.

as is usual with most eagles. During incubation the nest is kept well lined with green leaves, and they continue to be brought, with decreasing regularity, until the eaglet is six weeks old. The incubation period is a long one, 48 – 50 days in the only instance I have established with accuracy; this means that it is as long as that of the Crowned Eagle, a very much larger species. From first chipping of the shell, the eaglet has a long struggle before it is free of the egg; in 1962 it took three days to hatch, and at least two days in 1971.

The fledging period has two distinct parts to it which are closely linked to the eaglet's development, and parental attention is regulated accordingly. At three weeks of age the first feathers sprout through the down, and within two weeks they effectively cover the head and back, although the underparts and posterior remain downy. An eaglet as this stage is an amusing creature; it looks like a mature eagle whose rear end has forgotten to develop, and its appearance may be likened to a man meticulously clad in dinner dress who has forgotten to put his trousers on. The important point is that, once it has this covering of feathers, it no longer requires parental care, except for food to be delivered, and so the female is released from the nest to help her mate in the search for prey. I found that parental attention showed a decline from as early as three weeks, but there was no sharp change until the eaglet was five weeks old. During this first stage thirty-two hours' observation in 1971 showed that a parent was on the nest 70% of the time, while from after five weeks until the eaglet fledged at 109 days the parents were only on the nest 1,2% of the sixty-four hours observed.

Initially the downy eaglet is closely brooded by the female, or she shades it by crouching over it with her back feathers raised to permit maximum circulation of air to her body. When she sees the male approaching he is greeted with a guttural "hok, hok, hok" call, but it should be mentioned that the 1962 birds were far more vocal than the 1971 pair. Shortly afterwards he alights with the tip of a snake's tail protruding from his mouth, and she grasps this with her bill and pulls it out, both birds straining back during the process. Usually the male departs immediately, but sometimes he may stand on the nest for a while, and once he stayed for twenty-five minutes before leaving. The 1971 male was in all respects more attached to the nest than the male of the previous study, and this makes me fairly certain that a different bird was involved.

Apart from this one lengthy stay on the nest, he was also seen to bring green leaves twice, and he even shaded the eight day old eaglet for ten minutes. But his main function is to bring prey, a task in which he is not found wanting, and he keeps both the eaglet and the female supplied during the first thirty-five days. Presumably he eats his own requirements first at times, because some of the larger snakes were brought with the first third of their length missing. All the other species of eagles I have studied start feeding on their prey from the head downwards, so there is no reason to suppose that some snakes were deliberately decapitated to avoid venom being brought to the nest.

After the male's departure, the female tears off small pieces of snake which are carefully offered to the eaglet in a manner no different from that of other eagles.

132

The female Brown Snake Eagle returns with a small cobra . . .

. . . pauses for a while with it

. . . and then it is pulled from her crop by the nineteen day old eaglet.

133

This alighting study shows the underwing pattern of the Brown Snake Eagle.

Full air-brakes are applied as the Brown Snake Eagle alights.

The only complication is that nest lining occasionally adheres to the sticky flesh, and then she has to shake her head about vigorously so as to flick off the offending leaf. Once a snake was full of eggs which somehow managed to get scattered about so that the nest looked like a sago pudding. A five day old eaglet was seen to peck at the snake on which it was being fed, and at nineteen days it swallowed the whole of a small snake which was brought. It cannot cope with larger snakes on its own for a while yet, and the female still has to tear them up for it. Long, thin snakes can be swallowed by the time parental attention drops off at thirty-five days, but it may still need to have large snakes torn up for a week or two after this.

After the eaglet is left to its own devices, it may be thought that interest diminishes in the absence of the parents. Nothing could be further from the truth, and I have been more entertained by young Snake Eagles than by any other eaglets I have watched. I have already described the eaglet's amusing appearance at five weeks of age, but I omitted to mention the large yellow eyes which seem out of proportion to the rest of its body. The rapid change of the iris to yellow is a further point of interest, for it is dark brown on hatching. When it is left on its own at five weeks the eaglet is able to stand weakly, but it cannot walk round the nest with confidence for at least another two weeks. During walks prior to being sure of its balance it leans well forward, thus revealing its downy posterior. Once it made a few wing flaps at six weeks, but no really serious attempts were seen until it was nearly ten weeks old.

My spells in the hide were usually from 8 a.m. until about four or five o'clock in the afternoon, and I came to expect the delivery of prey between 11 a.m. and 3 p.m., the warmest part of the day when snakes were most likely to be caught. Although officially "winter", the days were warm and often hot, and quite clearly snakes were readily available. More surprising, however, was that on certain days, when the weather was overcast and extremely cold, snakes were still caught, which runs counter to the belief that they do not appear in cold weather. The eaglet would alert me for the delivery of prey by calling loudly, a hoarse "yak, yak, yak" made in solicitation with neck and back feathers raised and wings held out limply at its sides. At times it gave a false alarm by calling to other raptors overhead, usually Bateleurs. Once the parent had alighted on the branches near the nest, it adopted a submissive posture with its body held horizontal, at the same time making a soft "yeeee" call. Then the adult would jump onto the nest and perhaps hook out the snake with its foot, but usually, especially in the later stages of the fledging period, the eaglet would grab the protruding tail in its bill and strain back, gripping the snake with one foot once it was on its way out. The parent would strain back too, and one would then see that the small piece of protruding tail was the prelude to a Boomslang almost a metre long which appeared from the eagle's mouth like a magician's trick.

Once it was withdrawn, the eaglet mantled over the snake until the parent flew off. On this occasion, as was the case a number of times, the Boomslang was still writhing, so the eaglet "killed" it with its feet and made twisting pecks up and down its spine. This behaviour was clearly instinctive for it would certainly not have had any opportunity of seeing its parents take similar action. After a few exploratory nibbles, it grasped the head and began gulping down the sinuous meal. Again it knew instinctively that snakes were to be swallowed head first, and only once did I see one, a very small specimen, swallowed tail first.

I don't think that the fascination of watching the delivery and subsequent swallowing of a snake will ever wear off, and some of the meals consumed had to be seen to be believed. I remember particularly a section of cobra a metre long which must have belonged to a snake nearly two metres long originally. The eaglet swallowed this with many convulsive gulps and twisting movements of its bulging neck; I timed it, and found that the cobra disappeared at the rate of about 30 centimetres a minute. If one is unkind enough to disturb the eaglet with a shout in the middle of such a meal, it stares at the hide with its large yellow eyes, the snake hanging down like an elephant's trunk. An even more prodigious swallowing feat was a Puff Adder, a much thicker snake about 60 centimetres long, which was gulped down in five minutes. When lecturing on the Brown Snake Eagle I have noted murmurs and incredulous looks from some members of the audience when such incidents are described, but they are silenced when I project a cine film taken by my friend Vic Tuer showing a large Puff Adder being swallowed.

The long hours of the eaglet's day are remarkably inactive, even when it is only a week or so from fledging. Much of its time is spent lying down or sleeping, far more so than other eaglets at a similar stage of development. Its activities consist mainly of preening, stretching, sun-bathing with spread wings and peering intently over the nest edge at passing animals such as small buck. Even though there were frequently some good breezes, it rarely indulged in wing exercises. Sometimes it did a "wing-spread", which meant that it merely held its wings open on the wind for a while. Only on its 104th day was it seen to flap vigorously, and two days later, without any preparatory exercises, it surprised me by making a flight of a metre across the nest to the branches on the other side. It stayed on its new perch for a long while and then jumped back to the nest.

On its 108th day it made a few longer flights across the top of the nest tree, but it had not left the nest when I departed late in the evening. Returning at 9 a.m. on the morning of its 110th day, I saw it perched on a tree uphill from the nest. There had been no breeze so far that day, so I'm reasonably certain that it flew there at some time the previous day, which means that it fledged in 109 days, a period of much the same length as the Crowned Eagle and longer than that of both the Martial and Black Eagle, all of them much larger than the Brown Snake Eagle. This is the same period as obtained by Leslie Brown in Kenya, although the 1962 eaglet had flown earlier, between 97 – 101 days. The period is long for the size of the eagle, and I can think of no reason for it to be so protracted.

When I saw the eaglet perched near the nest on its 110th day I hid myself, and twenty minutes later it flew back to the nest when a breeze came up the valley. I made a cautious approach and entry into the hide, and it crouched flat on the nest on seeing me. Until I left at three o'clock it remained largely inactive, except for wing exercises on two occasions; had I arrived later that morning I would never

This series shows the delivery of a snake to the ninety-four day old eaglet: here it solicits loudly on sighting the adult in the distance.

The female Brown Snake Eagle arrives with only the tip of the snake's tail protruding.

The eaglet grasps the snake with its bill and foot.

138

Both the eaglet and the female strain back as the snake is withdrawn.

The female pauses before leaving while the eaglet mantles over the prey.

When she has left it commences to gulp down its sinuous meal – a Boomslang 94 centimetres long.

139

Some studies of the 104 day old Brown Snake Eagle: here it is on a favourite perch behind the nest.

It spreads its wings on a strong breeze but does not flap them.

140

With spread wings the eaglet sun-bathes.

A "flight" back to the nest from its perch.

141

have suspected that it had made its first flight. Interestingly, it was fed twice, at noon and at two-thirty. Although I had watched during the hours that prey was normally brought on its 104th, 106th and 108th day, it had not been fed at all, and the evidence suggests that it may be starved towards the end of the fledging period. When I made a quick visit the following afternoon it was on the nest and crouched as I approached, so I retired without disturbing it further.

Six days after its first flight I found a piece of Puff Adder on the nest which showed that it was still being brought food at that stage. Sixteen days after it fledged I watched the nest area for five hours, and the young eagle soared above the nest in competent fashion soon after my arrival at nine o'clock. Except for some white edges to the feathers of its breast and abdomen, it resembled its parents; in view of this similarity I had cut a small identification "window" between two primary feathers, and I was pleased to see that this showed up well. After a while it flew to perch on a tree a kilometre away where it remained until I left. The only interest was provided when a Black-breasted Snake Eagle made six spectacular dive-bomb attacks, wings folded and claws extended, from heights of 50 – 100 metres. On each occasion the young eagle ducked in time. Four days later I watched the nest in the evening until darkness fell, but I did not see the parents or the young eagle roosting anywhere in the vicinity. The picture of the post-fledging period, on present evidence, is one of a brief attachment to the nest area before abandoning it to range further afield.

It only remains to give a summary of the prey recorded during the two studies and, apart from one chameleon and a leguaan, all of the thirty-nine items of prey were snakes; eight Black-necked Cobras, seven Boomslangs, five Puff Adders, three Stripe-bellied Grass Snakes, one Burrowing Snake (a species of *Typhlops*) and thirteen unidentified snakes, many of them thought to be cobras. It should be pointed out that, unlike other eagles, prey remains did not usually lie about the nest for identification; snakes disappeared pretty promptly, especially once the eaglet could swallow prey whole. But one is left in little doubt that the change of name from Harrier-Eagle to Snake Eagle is a sound one.

Much as I enjoyed them, I was pleased when my observations drew to a successful conclusion, for they required a great deal of time, and this meant that my other eagle studies had to be neglected. I had started when the hills had been clad in a mantle of green grass and the nest tree was in full leaf; when I finished the arched backs of the hills were brown, and the nest surrounded by bare branches which would only bud and burst with new life again during the intense heat that ushered in the next rainy season.

I have seen six occupied Black-breasted Snake Eagle nests, four at Essexvale, one in the Matopos and another at Makarikari Pan in Botswana. The Matopos one, where I obtained a few pictures before the eaglet was stoned to death by local Africans, was on top of an euphorbia, but the others were all on flat-topped thorn trees at heights varying from four to six metres. All were slight structures that would not have been distinguishable, in the absence of the adult, from the nests of the Brown Snake Eagle. Indeed, as I have said, the breeding behaviour of the two species is very similar, and it would be repetitive to give details again.

142

The female Black-breasted Snake Eagle at her nest on top of a euphorbia in the Matopos.

My main study was of a single nest at Essexvale that I found with a fresh egg at the end of March 1963. The site was about five kilometres from the Brown Snake Eagle, and was similarly located on a hillside from which the nest could be overlooked. In this case the slope was sufficiently steep to obviate the need for a pylon hide, and a ground hide was all that was required. Only 300 metres from the nest there was an occupied African kraal, so I arranged with the headman there that I would pay him a reward if the eaglet flew successfully; one would be amazed at the items that find their way into a three-legged cooking pot, and I was anxious to insure against this possibility.

Although periods of observation were not as intensive as those on the Brown Snake Eagle, a clear picture of the breeding cycle emerged. Like that of the Brown, the incubation period was long, close on fifty days. The development of the eaglet was in advance of the Brown, first feathers showed through the down as early as two weeks and made an effective covering by four weeks, at which stage it could swallow smaller prey by itself. Parental care was regulated accordingly, and the sharp drop in attention was a week in advance of that of the Brown Snake Eagle. As may be expected, the fledging period was shorter too, and the eaglet flew when ninety days old. Few observations were made on post-fledging care on that occasion, but at another site a juvenile was still soliciting its parents for food six months after leaving the nest.

The method of prey delivery was no different from that of the Brown Snake Eagle, but generally smaller snakes were brought; it will be necessary to investigate further to establish whether the Black-breasted is unable to cope with snakes as big as the largest taken by the Brown, but it may well be that their smaller feet are the limiting factor. There were three toads or frogs amongst the fourteen items recorded, the only departure from reptilian prey noted for either species of Snake Eagle at Essexvale. If they prey on chickens, as they are said to do, then it is surprising that they did not help themselves to those which wandered freely about the kraal only a short distance away. Besides the amphibians and a single chameleon, I noted four Black-necked Cobras, three Puff Adders, one Boomslang, a Night Adder and an unidentified snake.

When the young eagle leaves the nest it is a uniform red-brown colour, unlike the dark brown of the Brown Snake Eagle, the only species with which it is likely to be confused. One year a nestling was brought to me by an African, who misguidedly thought that this was what I wanted when I spread the word that I would pay a reward for any eagle nests *shown* to me. It was too late to return the eaglet to the nest, so I reared it and had it about the garden for nearly two years. During this period it gave me valuable information on moult, and its new flight feathers showed the bold barring of the adult. The red-brown juvenile feathers were gradually replaced by grey-brown above, and by black feathers on the gorget. On the abdomen mottled white and brown feathers emerged, and the brown disappeared as the feathers began to wear. At this stage it was a ragged version of the adult, and it would probably have taken four years to assume full adult plumage. Unfortunately, it died in an accident before I could confirm this. While we had it, it was an amusing and useful

The female Brown Snake Eagle brings in a Yellow-bellied Grass Snake which is still writhing: only half the snake's length protrudes from her bill.

The female Black-breasted Snake Eagle returns to her nest with a Black-necked Cobra, half of which is swallowed. The small feet show up well in this picture.

pet. As it was my habit to wander around the garden barefoot, I was more than grateful when it saw and killed a Night Adder that emerged from a bed of zinnias near me as I was watering them one evening. It has never needed to learn how to deal with snakes, and did all the right things instinctively.

Perhaps what I enjoyed most about my Snake Eagle studies, and here I'm thinking particularly of the Brown Snake Eagle, was the solitude. This is a rare luxury these days, and it was almost as if it seeped into my being by a process of osmosis. Once the Land Rover was wheezing up that tortuous track, it was as though I were entering my private Avalon. In two periods of six months each spent in those lonely hills,

146

A Black-breasted Snake Eagle returns to its well concealed nest on top of a thorn tree.

A female Black-breasted Snake Eagle pulls a snake from the male's crop.

I saw one old white-haired African passing in the valley below. Occasionally, when the wind was right, the muffled shouts of cattle-herders carried across the hills behind me like disembodied voices from another world. And sometimes, from the depths of a distant valley, I heard the faint mellow clonk of a goat's bell like a noonday knell.

10 *The Bateleur*

As the Fish Eagle is the voice of Africa, so the Bateleur is lord of its skies. There cannot be many who have not thrilled at the sight of that purposeful silhouette sweeping across a panoramic expanse of savanna. The shape and graceful ease of flight are first to command our attention, and even those with only a passing interest in natural things are impressed. The Bateleur is indeed an eagle marvellous to behold, not least for its striking coloration, and with its short tail and long wings it is the avian prototype of the delta-winged aircraft. Those with a more discerning eye will note that male birds have a wide area of black at the hind edge of the white underwing, while females merely have a narrow black strip, a clear and easy distinction enabling one to recognise the sexes at a glance.

The Bateleur was given its name by Francois Le Vaillant, the French naturalist and explorer who travelled in southern Africa during the years 1781 – 1784, but the word has several interpretations, so we are not sure what feature he wished to stress. It can mean acrobat, tumbler or juggler, and it is thought that the name was intended to apply to its aerobatics on the wing. However, as anyone who has spent any length of time in the African bush will know, one rarely sees the Bateleur perform antics in flight. It is capable of remarkable 360 degree sideways rolls in quick succession, and it is stated to be able to clap its wings together, both above and below the body. I'm rather doubtful about reports of wing clapping, and think that this may be a misinterpretation of the "whoofing" noise produced by the rapid beats when it flaps to regain height or accelerate. But it is unwise to be dogmatic about the habits of birds, and Africans, who are usually astute observers, state that they do clap their wings. Another translation of Bateleur is tightrope walker, and if one visualizes the long swaying pole of the balancer as he maintains his equilibrium, then one is strongly reminded of the rocking flight of the Bateleur as it glides rapidly across country. This, to me, is the interpretation of its name which makes most sense, and it is the one I prefer.

Where the white man is moved to admiration of the Bateleur, the African is filled with awe. Consequently it features prominently in their folk-lore and superstitions, perhaps second only to the Hamerkop or *Tegwane*, as members of the Nguni group, amongst whom the Zulus are the most prominent tribe, call this dreaded species. My comments refer mainly to this linguistic group, but it is evident that these beliefs are common to most tribes in southern Africa. The usual name for the Bateleur amongst the Nguni speaking tribes is *ingqungqulu*, which means "warrior bird"; the name (if one can get one's tongue round the 'gq' clicks) is onomatopoeic, and suggests the sound of a knobkierie beating upon a rawhide shield. Various other names for the Bateleur have a warlike connotation, so it is not surprising that many beliefs about it concern fighting. The resonant "haa-aw" cry was thought to presage war, and the side over which it flew in battle was the one that would be defeated. In this latter regard the Bateleur was presumably only displaying a "professional" interest, as one of its names *indlamadoda* (the eater of the warriors) indicates. Even those beliefs not associated with warfare are not exactly cheerful; if it called above a traveller he should take immediate steps to protect himself from a disaster, over a village its cry was a portent of evil, and if the shadow of a flying bird covered you, then you would never again have full use of your senses. The Mashona people of Rhodesia, who call the Bateleur *chapungu*, consider that it carries the spirit of a departed one, usually a person of some importance such as a chief. On seeing it the men clap their hands, and the women perform ululations, beating their hands upon their mouths Red Indian style.

The beak and claws of a dead Bateleur are much prized by witchdoctors, indeed they are the only ones who would dare handle such things. Bateleurs are not molested, and their nests are usually left severely alone. The two African assistants I have had over the years would climb to nests, but they were emancipated from tribal beliefs, as are many of the younger men these days. Their older acquaintances, however, assured them that their effrontery would bring them to a sticky end.

The accuracy of observations by primitive Africans is revealed in two statements; "It does not want to drop and lose a single feather" and "It is a marvellous bird, for, no matter where it is, it would know if you touched its nest". These comments refer to the very gradual process of moult, so that one rarely sees a Bateleur missing a wing feather, and to its extreme wariness at the nest, a subject which I shall touch on later.

Most people think of the Bateleur mainly as an eater of carrion, which is an important part of its diet, but less known is that, like the Tawny and Fish Eagles, it is a pirate too; a friend of mine once saw a pair drive a soaring Martial Eagle almost to the ground after repeated diving attacks. The Bateleur also kills live prey, including snakes such as the Puff Adder. These are carried, if being conveyed to a nest, in the manner of Snake Eagles which, coupled with other factors, supports the suggestion that the Bateleur is most closely related to this group. At nests at Essexvale I recorded a wide variety of mammalian prey, much of it probably derived as carrion, as well as a few fish and some snakes. The fish were probably stranded in drying pools, or found already dead.

But the most interesting aspect was the high proportion of birds I recorded, and it seems that I was first to draw attention to the extent to which avian prey features as part of the Bateleur's diet, at least while they have a youngster in the nest. During the preliminary years of my study I visited nests at Essexvale as often as possible, although some sites involved considerable travel. Eventually fifty-eight prey items were gathered, and of these 41% were birds. Subsequently, during a further seven years of observation, I was able to confirm that birds were regularly brought to nests. They ranged in size from the Crowned Guineafowl to species as small as the Brown-hooded Kingfisher and Crimson-breasted Shrike. Francolins, hornbills, plovers, doves, nightjars, Grey Loeries, Lilac-breasted Rollers, glossy starlings and various other

150

A Bateleur is artistically framed by the branches of a dead tree in the Chobe Game Reserve.

species were recorded. Except for the nightjars, which are regular road casualties, I can not accept that most of these birds were found dead. My contention is strengthened by the fact that others have now found that birds form an important part of the Bateleur's diet, and I refer here particularly to unpublished research carried out in the Kruger Park and the Kalahari Gemsbok Park. The evidence strongly suggests that live birds are regularly taken, and I have stuck my neck out and suggested that these may even be killed in flight at times. If one has seen a Bateleur stoop at full speed, then this claim ceases to be remarkable. Imagine a hornbill dipping its way across an open stretch of country and intercepted by a Bateleur – it would be like a First World War plane being pursued by a modern jet fighter.

At Essexvale I was able to study the breeding history of one pair over a period of eight years, and I supplemented my observations with visits to several other sites on a somewhat desultory basis. The male of my main study pair was easy to identify by his behaviour, and this confirmed that I was dealing with the same pair when they moved to new nest sites. At certain stages of the nesting period, particularly when there was a small chick in the nest, he would "do his thing". This consisted of alighting on a prominent perch near the nest where he adopted a crouching position; then he would flap his wings about limply, at the same time giving a chattering "ka, ka, ka, ka" call. During this performance he would permit me to walk up to within nine metres of him before taking flight. Other observers have described an aggressive display, during which the body is jerked up and down to the accompaniment of sharp barks. One description of the call was, "cursing me, two barks to the second". I found it difficult to equate the male's behaviour and call with these accounts, and the impression I obtained was that he was deliberately attempting to draw my attention from the nest. Furthermore, it may not be too far-fetched to suggest that the limp flapping of his wings was akin to the feigning of injury performed by ground-nesting birds such as plovers, especially in view of the close approach he permitted me to make. My claim has not been warmly received by the pundits, because eagles are not supposed to perform distraction displays, but it should be borne in mind that the Bateleur differs markedly from other raptors in its "psychological" make-up.

But while we may argue over my interpretation of this aspect of his behaviour, the spectacular stoops he made when the nest tree was climbed left no doubt about his aggressive intent. He would fly in a wide arc and line up on the nest tree before diving at an increasing speed until he swept low overhead with a whoosh like a jet aircraft; then he soared up high into the sky with the momentum, his chestnut back catching the sun. One of my pupils baited him once by sticking his head out of the tree top, and but for his timely ducks there is no doubt that he would have been struck. I took Dr. Walter Spofford, an American ornithologist, to witness these spectacular dives and he was deeply impressed. Once, when the young bird had only just made its first flight, the male was particularly aggressive, and he began dive-bombing us as we were approaching the nest a kilometre away. In sharp contrast to the behaviour of her mate, the female was very wary at all times, and she rarely came anywhere near the nest while we were there.

152

The male Bateleur "doing his thing", a probable distraction display: here he calls and flaps his wings limply.

Another position with head hanging down and still calling.

153

The extreme wariness of the Bateleur at the nest is quite different from the behaviour of all other eagles I know, and it should be pointed out that although the male was demonstrative near the nest, he would not return to it until observers were well away from the area. Even a newly hatched chick will be left unattended if the parents are in the least bit suspicious; at such a time other eagles are generally very tame. This means that any attempt to build a hide results in almost certain desertion, and photographers should refrain from making attempts to get pictures at the nest. It is reasonably easy to get telephoto pictures of a perched bird in most Game Reserves, and once in the Chobe Game Reserve I found a gathering of twenty Bateleurs which regularly congregated on dead trees at a particular bend in the river which I named "Bateleur Bay". The birds were in all plumages from brown juveniles (which take seven years to adult plumage) to "sooty" sub-adults. There was even an adult with a creamy back instead of the normal chestnut, a colour variation which is occasionally encountered, and there is still doubt whether this represents genuine polymorphism or is merely an indication of a very old bird. Another way of obtaining pictures of the Bateleur is to attract it to carrion, and it is a method I intend to try.

When built by itself the nest of the Bateleur is not large, much the same size as that of a Wahlberg's Eagle, but it quite often takes over and repairs the old nests of other eagles. Large trees are preferred, often those along a river or dry watercourse, and the nest is situated within the canopy. A single large white egg is laid, and the incubation period in one case I recorded was not less than 52 days. Protracted watches were prevented by the wariness of the birds, but the male at the nest of my main study was flushed off a number of times during incubation, and the circumstantial evidence suggested that he did a substantial share of this duty.

The newly hatched eaglet is the most delightful of all the eagles I have studied, and its large creamy-buff head is offset against the dark brown of its back. I made a full study of an eaglet's development in one year, and the most interesting feature was the similarity to the Snake Eagles in the rapid development of feathers on the head and back. When half grown the eaglet has a fully developed head, at the back of which it raises an impressive ruff of feathers if annoyed. When fully grown it is superficially similar to the young Brown Snake Eagle, but its short tail and brown eyes serve to distinguish it. One year, by concealing myself over 300 metres from a nest, I was able to establish that both sexes fed the eaglet, the male even tearing up prey and giving it small pieces.

In the only fledging period I obtained with accuracy, the eaglet left on its 111th or 112th day, and records by other observers confirm that the period is a long one. Post-fledging attachment to the nest varies; sometimes the juvenile does not come back at all, while at other nests prey remains indicated that young birds returned for several weeks after their first flight. Once I found that a youngster recently out of the nest had adopted a perch two kilometres away, where I saw it on a number of occasions. On my approach it would crouch across a bare branch in an attempt to look as inconspicuous as possible, only flying off when I was nearly up to it. Soaring away it became a creature of grace, where a moment before it had merely looked ridiculous.

A Bateleur chick raises its impressive crest.

155

A creamy-backed Bateleur photographed in the Chobe Game Reserve.

With its creamy head and chocolate-brown body this two day old Bateleur chick is an attractive creature.

At three weeks old it resembles a bizarre child's toy.

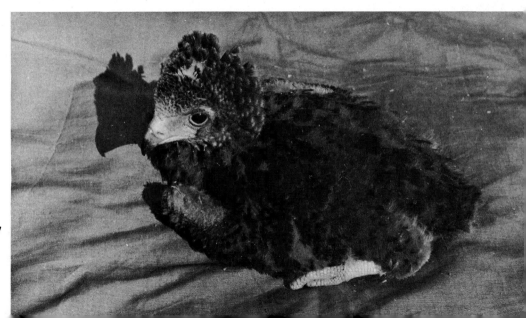

The feather development of the six week old chick shows close similarities to that of the Snake Eagles.

157

A male Bateleur sweeps through the sky.

There is clear evidence that the Bateleur is not as widely distributed in South Africa as it used to be, particularly in the Cape Province. Many of the instances of folk-lore to which I referred earlier emanated from the Eastern Cape, but the Bateleur is now rare or extinct there in areas where it was formerly known to occur. In Rhodesia the Bateleur is still plentiful, and one rarely spends a day in the bush without seeing several. Long may this continue, for if ever the sky under which I walk ceases to be graced by the magnificence of a flying Bateleur, then the sun will have set on my eagle days.

GLOSSARY

(MAINLY FOR READERS OUTSIDE AFRICA)

ALATES – in the context of this book the winged form of termites as they emerge from their nests on their nuptial flight. Termites are an extremely nutritious food source eaten by many birds, the Steppe Eagle being one of the largest to do so.

BOOMSLANG – the common name, from Afrikaans, for the tree-snake *Dispholidus typus*. The venom of this back-fanged species causes severe internal bleeding which may prove fatal.

CERE – the fleshy covering on the upper mandible at its junction with the head, a feature found in all birds of prey.

COMMIPHORA – the Paper Tree *Commiphora marlothii* from the succulent trunk of which a brittle "paper" bark flakes off. The Ndebele name "mpapapa" is onomatopoeic and suggests the sound of the "paper" flapping in the wind.

DASSIE – the common name, from Afrikaans, for a hyrax, also sometimes erroneously called a Rock "Rabbit". The Rock Dassie *Procavia capensis* is the species most often taken by the Black Eagle in southern Africa, but the Yellow-spotted Dassie *Heterohyrax brucei* is also preyed upon, especially in the Matopos.

HAEMANTHUS – the Blood Flower or Snake Lily which belongs to the Amaryllis family. It grows from a bulb, and the striking red "puffball" flower usually appears after the first rains.

KLOOF – a deep valley, usually flanked by cliffs.

KNOBKIERIE – a sturdy stick with a heavy knob at the end. Used in African tribal wars to good effect to beat an opponent's brains out.

KRAAL – in the context of this book a small village of African huts.

LECHWE – the antelope *Kobus lechwe*.

LEGUAAN – a Monitor lizard; the species referred to in Chapters 2 and 9 is *Varanus niloticus*.

MASHONA – the main tribe inhabiting the northern part of Rhodesia, called Mashonaland, and centred on Salisbury.

MATABELE – the main tribe of the southern portion of Rhodesia called Matabeleland. The Matabele are an offshoot of the Zulus and were established in Rhodesia when Mzilikazi fled from Zululand during a period of internecine strife. He settled near present-day Bulawayo.

MIST-NET – a fine mesh, usually made of black nylon, used by bird-ringers to capture birds.

NDEBELE – the language of the Matabele.

NGUNI – a linguistic group made up of those southern African tribes whose language is characterized by the presence of click sounds. Such tribes as the Zulus, Swazis, Xhosas, Fingoes and Matabeles belong to this group.

PLATANNA – common name, from Afrikaans, for the frog *Xenopus laevis*. The name originally derives from "Plathander" which means flat hands.

SIBLING – in the context of this book an eaglet's "brother" or "sister".

TARN – a small lake in the mountains.

VLEI – Afrikaans for a lake, or a low-lying area inundated during the rainy season.

BIBLIOGRAPHY

GENERAL SOURCES

The following references are applicable to all or most chapters in the book and are listed here to avoid needless repetition under each chapter.

BROWN, L. H. 1953. On the Biology of the Large Birds of Prey of Embu District, Kenya Colony. *Ibis* 95:74–114.

BROWN, L. H. 1955. Supplementary Notes on the Biology of the Large Birds of Prey of Embu District, Kenya Colony. *Ibis* 97:38–64.

BROWN, L. 1955. *Eagles*. Michael Joseph:London.

BROWN, L. H. 1966. Observations on Some Kenya Eagles. *Ibis* 108:531–572.

BROWN, L. & AMADON, D. 1968. *Eagles, Hawks and Falcons of the World*. Country Life Books, Hamlyn Publishing Group; Feltham.

BROWN, L. 1970. *Eagles*. Arthur Barker: London.

BROWN, L. 1970. *African Birds of Prey*. Collins; London.

COATES PALGRAVE, O. H. 1957. *Trees of Central Africa*. National Publications Trust:Salisbury.

MCLACHLAN, G. R. & LIVERSIDGE, R. 1970. *Roberts Birds of South Africa*. C.N.A.:Cape Town.

THOMSON, A. LANDSBOROUGH (Editor). 1964. *A New Dictionary of Birds*. Thomas Nelson:London.

STEYN, P. 1971. The Diurnal Birds of Prey. *In Birdlife in Southern Africa* (ed. K. Newman). Purnell & Sons: Johannesburg.

SPECIFIC CHAPTER SOURCES

These are the main sources applicable to the individual chapters. Many of them may be used on a "snowball" basis, for example my paper on the Tawny Eagle in Chap. 5 lists 51 further references.

Chapter 1.

GARGETT, V. 1967. Black Eagle Experiment. *Bokmakierie* 19:88–90.

GARGETT, V. 1970. Black Eagle Survey, Rhodes Matopos National Park. A Population Study 1964–1968. *Ostrich* Suppl. 8:397–414.

GARGETT, V. 1970. Black Eagle Experiment No. 2. *Bokmakierie* 22:32–35.

GARGETT, V. 1971. Nature's Way. *Bokmakierie* 23:16–17.

GARGETT, V. 1971. Observations on the Black Eagles in the Matopos, Rhodesia. *Ostrich* Suppl. 9:91–124.

GARGETT, V. 1972. Observations at a Black Eagle Nest in the Matopos, Rhodesia. *Ostrich* 43:77–108.

GARGETT, V. 1972. Black Eagle Survey:Report for the 1972 Breeding Season. Rhodesian Ornithological Society – Matabeleland Branch.

GARGETT, V. 1972. Black Eagles in the Matopos. *African Wildlife* 26:12–17.

ROWE, E. G. 1947. The Breeding Biology of *Aquila verreauxi* Lesson. *Ibis* 89:387 – 410 and 576 – 606.

VERNON, C. J. 1965. The 1964 Black Eagle Survey in the Matopos, Rhodesia. *Arnoldia* 2(6):1–9.

VERNON, C. J. 1967. Birds of the Matopos, Rhodesia. *S.A. Avifauna Series No. 48.* P.F.I.A.O.:Cape Town.

Chapter 2.

BROWN, L. 1959. *The Mystery of the Flamingos.* Country Life:London.

BROWN, L. H. 1960. The African Fish Eagle *Haliaetus vocifer*, especially in the Kavirondo Gulf. *Ibis* 102:285–287.

GAITSKELL, H. 1970. Impasse. *The Hartebeest* 2:48.

STEYN, P. 1960. Observations on the African Fish Eagle. *Bokmakierie* 12:21–28.

STEYN, P. 1972. African Fish Eagle: A Record of Breeding Success. *Ostrich* 43:181–182

Chapter 3.

BROWN, L. H. & WATSON, A. 1964. The Golden Eagle in Relation to its Food Supply. *Ibis* 106:78–100.

BROWN, L. H. 1969. Status and Breeding Success of the Golden Eagles in North-West Sutherland in 1967. *British Birds* 62(9):345–363

GORDON, S. 1955. *The Golden Eagle.* Collins:London.

PETERSON, R., MOUNTFORT, G. & HOLLOM, P. A. D. 1959. *A Field Guide to the Birds of Britain and Europe.* Collins:London.

Chapter 4.

BROWN, L. H. 1971. Some Factors Affecting Breeding in Eagles. *Ostrich* Suppl. 8:157–167.

SELOUS, F. C. 1896. *Sunshine and Storm in Rhodesia.* Rowland Ward:London.

SIEGFRIED, W. R. 1968. Breeding Season, Clutch and Brood Sizes in Verreaux's Eagle. *Ostrich* 39:139–145.

SMITHERS, R. H. N., STUART IRWIN, M. P. & PATERSON, M. L. 1957. *A Check List of the Birds of Southern Rhodesia.* Rhodesian Ornithological Society; Cambridge University Press.

SNELLING, J. C. 1971. Some Information Obtained from Marking Large Raptors in Kruger National Park, Republic of South Africa. *Ostrich* Suppl. 8:415–427.

STEYN, P. 1962. Observations on Wahlberg's Eagle. *Bokmakierie* 14:7–14.

Chapter 5.

BROOKE, R. K., GROBLER, J. H., STUART IRWIN, M. P. & STEYN, P. 1972. A study of the Migratory Eagles *Aquila nipalensis* and *A. pomarina* (Aves; Accipitridae) in Southern Africa, with Comparitive Notes on other Large Raptors. *Occ. Pap. Natn. Mus. Rhod.* B5(2):61–114.

JENSEN, R.A.C. 1972. The Steppe Eagle *Aquila nipalensis* and Other Termite-eating Raptors in South West Africa. *Madoqua* Ser. 1 No. 5:73 – 76.

STEYN, P. 1973. Observations on the Tawny Eagle *Ostrich* 44:1–22.

Chapter 6.

BROWN, L. H. 1966. Observations on Some Kenya Eagles. *Ibis* 108:545–571.

BROWN, L. H. 1971. The Relations of the Crowned Eagle *Stephanoaetus coronatus* and some of its Prey Animals. *Ibis* 113:240–243.

STEYN, P. 1964. The Crowned Eagle at Home. *African Wildlife* 18:95–101.

Chapter 7.

KNIGHT, C. W. R. 1937. *Knight in Africa.* Country Life:London.

SIEGFRIED, W. R. 1963. A Preliminary Report on the Black and Martial Eagles in the Laingsburg and Philipstown Divisions. *Investigational Report No. 5.* Dept. of Nat. Conserv.: Prov. Admin. of Cape of Good Hope.

Chapter 8.

See under BROWN in General Sources.

Chapter 9.

FITZSIMONS, V. F. M. 1962. *Snakes of Southern Africa.* Purnell & Sons:Johannesburg.

STEYN, P. 1964. Observations on the Brown Snake Eagle. *Ostrich* 35:22–31.

STEYN, P. 1966. Observations on the Black-breasted Snake Eagle. *Ostrich* Suppl. 6:141–154.

STEYN, P. 1972. Further Observations on the Brown Snake Eagle. *Ostrich* 43:149–164.

Chapter 10.

BROWN, L. H. & CADE, T. J. 1972. Age Classes and Population Dynamics of the Bateleur and African Fish Eagle. *Ostrich* 43:1–16.

GODFREY, R. 1941. *Bird-Lore of the Eastern Cape Province.* "Bantu Sudies". Monograph Series No. 2. Witwatersrand University Press.

MOREAU, R. E. 1945. On the Bateleur, especially at the Nest. *Ibis* 87:224–249.

SKEAD, C. J. 1967. Ecology of Birds in the Eastern Cape Province. *Ostrich* Suppl. 7:60.

STEYN, P. 1965. Some Observations on the Bateleur. *Ostrich* 36:203–213.

SCIENTIFIC NAMES

Wandering Albatross	*Diomeda exulans*
Storm Petrel	*Hydrobates pelagicus*
Cattle Egret	*Bubulcus ibis*
Hamerkop	*Scopus umbretta*
Pygmy Goose	*Nettapus auritus*
Secretary Bird	*Sagittarius serpentarius*
Cape Vulture	*Gyps coprotheres*
White-headed Vulture	*Trigonoceps occipitalis*
Peregrine Falcon	*Falco peregrinus*
Lanner Falcon	*Falco biarmicus*
Rock Kestrel	*Falco tinnunculus*
Black-shouldered Kite	*Elanus caeruleus*
Golden Eagle	*Aquila chrysaetos*
Black Eagle	*Aquila verreauxi*
Tawny Eagle	*Aquila rapax*
Steppe Eagle	*Aquila nipalensis*
Lesser Spotted Eagle	*Aquila pomarina*
Wahlberg's Eagle	*Aquila wahlbergi*
Long-crested Eagle	*Lophaetus occipitalis*
Ayres' Hawk-Eagle	*Hieraaetus dubius*
African Hawk-Eagle	*Hieraaetus spilogaster*
Martial Eagle	*Polemaetus bellicosus*
Crowned Eagle	*Stephanoaetus coronatus*
Brown Snake Eagle	*Circaetus cinereus*
Black-breasted Snake Eagle	*Circaetus pectoralis*
Southern Banded Snake Eagle	*Circaetus fasciolatus*
Banded Snake Eagle	*Circaetus cinerascens*
Fish Eagle	*Haliaetus vocifer*
Lammergeyer (Bearded Vulture)	*Gypaetus barbatus*
Bateleur	*Terathopius ecaudatus*
Jackal Buzzard	*Buteo rufofuscus*
Red-breasted Sparrowhawk	*Accipiter rufiventris*
African Goshawk	*Accipiter tachiro*
Gymnogene	*Polyboroides typus*
Osprey	*Pandion haliaetus*
Coqui Francolin	*Francolinus coqui*
Red-billed Francolin	*Francolinus adspersus*
Swainson's Francolin	*Francolinus swainsoni*
Crowned Guineafowl	*Numida meleagris*
Coot	*Fulica cristata*
Black-bellied Korhaan	*Lissotis melanogaster*
Wattled Plover	*Afribyx senegallus*
Common Sandpiper	*Actitis hypoleucos*
Curlew	*Numenius arquata*
Common Gull	*Larus canus*
Grey Loerie	*Corythaixoides concolor*
Klaas' Cuckoo	*Chrysococcyx klaas*
Barn Owl	*Tyto alba*
Spotted Eagle Owl	*Bubo africanus*
Giant Eagle Owl	*Bubo lacteus*
Rufous-checked Nightjar	*Caprimulgus rufigena*
Horus Swift	*Apus horus*
Malachite Kingfisher	*Corythornis cristata*
Brown-hooded Kingfisher	*Halcyon albiventris*
Lilac-breasted Roller	*Coracias caudata*
White-fronted Bee-eater	*Melittophagus bullockoides*
Red-billed Hoopoe	*Phoeniculus purpureus*
Bearded Woodpecker	*Thripias namaquus*
Fork-tailed Drongo	*Dicrurus adsimilis*
Black-headed Oriole	*Oriolus larvatus*
Pied Crow	*Corvus albus*
Raven	*Corvus corax*
White-necked Raven	*Corvultur albicollis*
Dipper	*Cinclus cinclus*
Paradise Flycatcher	*Terpsiphone viridis*
Crimson-breasted Shrike	*Laniarius atro-coccineus*
Yellow-throated Sparrow	*Petronia superciliaris*
Red-headed Weaver	*Anaplectes rubriceps*

INDEX

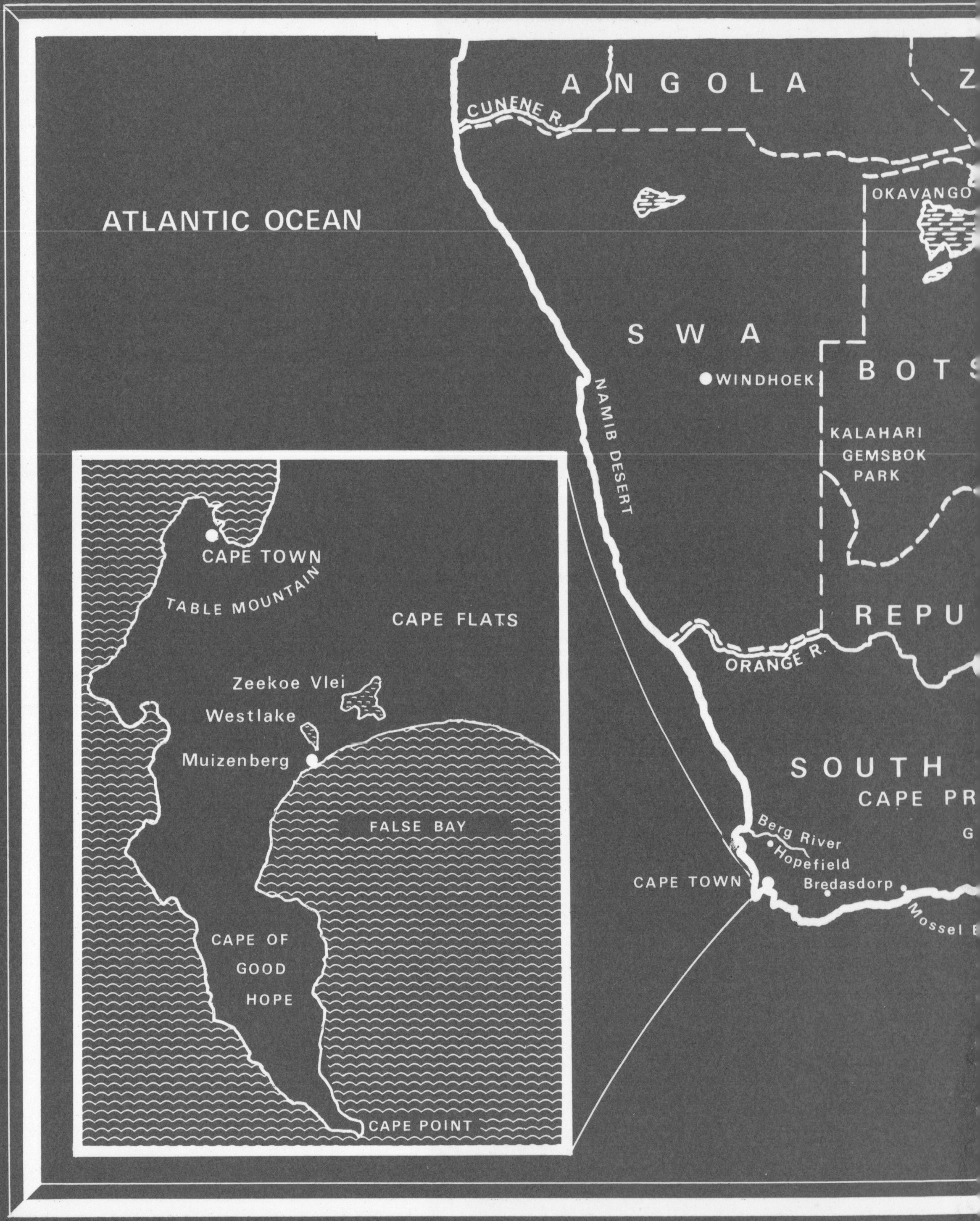
ANGOLA
Z
CUNENE R.
OKAVANGO
ATLANTIC OCEAN
SWA
WINDHOEK
BOTS
NAMIB DESERT
KALAHARI GEMSBOK PARK
REPU
ORANGE R.
SOUTH
CAPE PR
G
Berg River
Hopefield
CAPE TOWN
Bredasdorp
Mossel B
CAPE TOWN
TABLE MOUNTAIN
CAPE FLATS
Zeekoe Vlei
Westlake
Muizenberg
FALSE BAY
CAPE OF GOOD HOPE
CAPE POINT